For Stephanie, Peter and Lincoln
For Louis
For Norma

ISBN: 978-0-578-56436-4

Acknowledgments
are due to the editors of the following journals, in which
a number of these poems first appeared.

All the Sins
Cagibi
Gravel
Hidden Channel
Illuminations
Iodine
A Lonely Riot
Ninth Letter
Offcourse
The Pangolin Review

Picaroon Poetry
Poetry Leaves
SNReview
Soft Cartel
StepAway
Tales from the Forest
Taxicab
Temenos
West Texas Literary Review
Zymbol

Printed and bound in the United States by Sheridan
sheridan.com

Elkhound Publications
Gracie Station Box 1453
New York, NY 10028
elkhound460@gmail.com

Finding
Americas

Finding Americas

George Ryan

ELKHOUND
NEW YORK

CONTENTS

Midtown Ecology

1

Bryant Park, 1
Woman Speaking on Bus, 1
Moth, 1
Late Afternoon, 2
Afternoon, Central Park, 2
Bells, 2
Deal, 3
Nocturne, from a Window, 3
Your Right Nipple, 4
Central Park, Early March, 4
Rooftop Lullaby, 5
Gulls, 5
A Name, 6
Interrupted by Dawn, 6
Wasp, 7
The Lady in the Lake, 7
A Visitor?, 8
In a Midtown Post Office, 9

2

Sunday Evening, July, 10
Early Lunch, 11
On a Flight of Steps, 12
Takeover, 13
Bank of Elevators, 14
Heat, Vistas, the Source, Pacific, 14
Rooftop, 15
Jones Beach, September, 15
Bus Stop, January, 16
111 Mott Street, 16
Bag in Tree, 16
Frontier Life, 17
New York City, 1904, 17

3

Midtown Ecology, 18
She Thinks Back, 18
Near Rhinebeck, 19
Photos from Space, 19
Unseen Passenger, 20
Signals, 21
Nude, 22
Christmas on Third Avenue, 22

Tapeworm, 22
Ramadan, 23
Ark, 23
Mourning Dove, 24
Message Received, 24
A Warm Evening, 25
A Visitor by Night, 25
Thief, 26
Bouquet, 27
Three Dialogues, 27
Linden, 29
Grass and Stuff, 29
Twitch, 30
Out There, 30
Interrupted Call, 31
A Landmark Gone, 32
Last Wish, 32
A Sight to See, 33
Halloween, 33
Get Yourself a Dog, 34
Ill Wind, 34

4
Hospital Floor, 35
View, 35
Independence Day on the Hudson River, 36
Warning Geese, 36
Me and the Mob, 37
Style, 37
Woman with a Question, 38
Goethe House Recital, 39
On the Side of a Building, 40
Three Storm Warnings, 40
Banner and Drums, 41
Taxi on Lexington, 42
Good Morning, 43
Unidentified Saint, 44
Only a Wavelength Away, 44
Westward, 45
On the Way Up, 46
A Ferrari, 46
Enlarged Detail, 47
First Anniversary of Twin Towers, 47
Why Are You Walking?, 48
Shower, 49
Live Performance, 49
Quandary, 50
It Can't Be Here, 50

Obituary, 51
A Drive in the Country, 52
Francois, 53
Ask Not, 53
Greenwood Men, 54
I Hate to Say It, 55
Thinking of Home, 55

5
Subway Passenger, 56
On Their Way, 56
Not This Relic, 57
Encounter, 57
Crossing a Street, 58
Hudson River Solitaire, Near Rhinecliff, 58
Label, 59
Comfort Shopping, 59
No Sixpack, 60
Outside a Building, 60
A Detail from Reality, 61
Waiting to Cross the Street, 61
Joke as Poem, 62
The Dark Side, 62
What Can We Do?, 62
Subway Foam, 63
Cawk Spoke Squawk, 63
A God Offended, 64
Star Trek Encounter, 65
Weaving Car, 66
Singing Woman, 66

Streets and Avenues

1
A Pianist's Departure, 67
Inward Eye, 67
Conjuror, 68
Migrating Butterfly, 68
Supermarket Incident, 69
Memorial at First and 49th, 69
Patient Break, 69
Couples, 70
Telephones, 72
A Lesson in Pricing, 72
Generations, 73
In a Crosstown Bus, 73
In Brooklyn, 74
By the Wayside, 75

Advice to the Police Academy, 76
Pedestrian Crossing, 77
Knock on This Door, 78
November, 78
Sweet Assassin, 79
Sorting Mail, 80
Response, 80

2
Like It Is, 81
Underground, 82
Surprised by Gulls, 82
Throwing Out a Bookcase, 83
Late Afternoon, First and 88th, 84
April Is Here, 84
Hospital Tomatoes, 85
Try Lourdes, 86
Neighbor, 86
Untitled, 87
Thieves, 87
Daybreak, 88
Before Dawn, 88
East River Views, 89

3
Volunteer, 91
New Year Awakening, 91
Radio Timer Accidentally Set, 92
In Passing, 92
Out of Touch, 93
Strange People in Subways, 94
AARP: 99 Great Ways to Save!, 94
Star Performer, 95
Headline, 95
Suspicion, 96
Shopping Cart Traveler, 96
Taking Off from JFK, 97
Auden on Lower East Side, 98
On First Hearing Frank O'Hara, 98
What to See in NYC, 99
Redhook, 100
Beetle, 100
Looking Out the Window, 101

4
At Times Square on New Year's Eve, 102
Must Sign, 102
A Cautionary Tale, 103

For Two Voices, 104
Mickey Rooney on Broadway, 106
Manhattan Geese, 106
Hen, 107
At the Metropolitan Museum of Art, 107
Backyard Parties, 109
Elegy in McDonald's, 109
Royal Visit, 110

5
Shirt Pocket, 111
Tweed, 112
Nothing to Declare, 113
Fifteenth Day of Christmas, 113
Spring, 114
Country Music Radio on Mother's Day, 115
Breaking News, 115
Recent Advances, 116
A Couple, 116
Street Sensitivity, 117
Drama, 118
Doorbell, 119
Reality, 119
Errant Son, 120
Sudden Recall, 120
Coal, 121
Cats in the Way, 122
By Ear, 122
Instructions, 123
Bacall, 123
BBC World News, 124
Poor Men Fishing, 124
This Painting, 125
In the Words of Joel Oppenheimer, 125
Fantasy, 126
Free Cake, 127

Before Midnight

1
Who You Need to Start a Riot, 128
Fellow Passenger, 129
Given a Lift, 129
My Opposite, 130
Kevorkian, 131
Gallery Opening, 131
A Poem Unread, 132
Maximum Security, 132

Going, 133
War Story, 133
At the National Enquirer, 134
Weekend Workers, 135
Metamorphosis, 135
Health Watch, 136
First Avenue, 137
Airport Surveillance, 138

2
Fireball, 139
The World at Work, 140
Who Goes There?, 140
At Night, 141
Between A and B, 141
Founding Publisher, 142
No Title, 142
Screams, 143
Legacy, 144
Notice, 144
Socialists and Others, 145
Memory, 145
On Wheels, 146
Bagel Place, 146
Alert, 147
Workout, 147
Old Man's Pride, 148
Provender, 148
Close Call, 149
Paddleboarder on East River, 149
Ladies, 150
In Years to Come, 150
Listening, 151
No Sign of Willie, 151
Photo Edit, 151
Regular Shampoo, 152

3
In Transit, 153
Dairy Aisle, 153
Hard Landing, 153
A Word to the Wise, 154
Curbside, 154
For Her, 154
Before Midnight, 155
Don't Walk, 155
Woman on Third & 85th, 156
Ad, 156

Dangerous People, 157
MRI, 157
Grapes, 158
Beans, 158
Marathon, 159
What Women Ignore, 160
Talk of Love, 160
A Question in Passing, 161
Maple, 161
At Two in the Afternoon, 161
Gone, 162
Card, 162
Heads, 163
Street Find, 163
Bat Attack, 164
Passing Through, 164
From Waterside, 165
Woodcock, 165
Cortege, 165
Still Around, 166
Moth-Eaten, 166
Who Reads My Poems?, 167

4
Central Park Reservoir, 168
Mina, 168
Directions for a Driver, 169
Spring Day, 169
Fortune, 170
A Place Name, 170
Gliding, 171
Busy Streets, 171
Main Entrance, 172
Times Square Honeybees, 172
Em and En, 173
Students, 173
Overheard, 173
Tall Fin, 174
Test, 174
Cement, 175
Containers, 175
Dinosaurs, 176
A Window Shade, 176
A Vacant Lot, 177
Woman Downtown, 177
Gladioli, 177
Away from Town, 178
Secure in Its Remoteness, 179

Police Academy, 179
Housework, 179
Conflict, 180
Emergency Room, 180

Americas

1
From Webster's Third New International Dictionary, 181
Push, 182
Blue Sky, 182
The Semidomesticated, 182
Who? What?, 183
Have You Written?, 183
Pray for It, 183
Astronaut, 184
Leaves, 184
The Witch and Daffodil, 185
Five Miniatures, 187

2
Phantom Infant, 188
Mariner Lost, 188
Need, 189
Walk, 189
Crawl, 190
A Slight Edge, 191
Moons, 192
Say It with Flowers, 192
Pen Name, 193
Her Walk, 193
Early Morning Baudelaire, 194
Clouds, 194
Going Back, 194

3
Nocturne, 195
Snowscape, 195
New England Graveyard Invaded by Trees, 196
Peaceable Kingdom, 197
Equinox, 197
Old People Wandering, 198
To My Daughter, 198
Newlyweds, 199
You Canoe, 199
Afloat, 200
Pissarro in Massachusetts, 201
Stanley Kunitz Gardening, 202

Winter Field, 202
Tour, 203
Photo Opportunity, 203
Alpacas, 204
In North Egremont, 205
Nauset Beach, 206
Winged Spirit, 206
Early Summer Mornings, 207
In a Strange Land, 208
First Snowman, 208
Some New England Butterflies, 209

4

Savannah in July, 210
Headstones with an Irish Name, 210
Alligator, 211
Egrets, 211
Distant Funnel, 212
Hothouse Geraniums, 212
Portavant Indian Mound, 213
Jeff Climbs Out and Walks Away, 213
Alabama, 1964, 214
Country Traffic, 215
Statue, 215
Perennial Weed, 216
Eastern Shore, 216
Inside Looking Out, Outside Looking In, 217

5

Indian Guide, 218
His Uncle, 219
Family Visit, 220
War Cry, 221
Protest, 221
An Anthropologist Comes Full Circle, 222
Before Intercontinental Missiles, 223
In Gallup, 224
September 6, 225

6

Lake Shore, 226
The Feast of St. Filomena, 226
Looking for Walter, 227
Shop Talk, 228
The Joy of Gardening, 228
Hate Groups, 229
A Long Ride North, 230
Overcast, 231

7

Delta Flight 708, 232
Redeye Window Seat, 233
Repellent, 234
Ellington in Iowa, 234
In Search of Polygamists, 235
A Lone Flamingo, 236
Fun Bison Facts, 237
Arizona Afternoon, 237
Mogollon Rim, 238
Real-World Scene, 238

8

Ruby Beach, 239
Impression, 239
Friday, 240
Northwest Forest, 240
Urban Problem, 241
Ponderosa, 241
Elephant Seals in California, 242
Home and Castle, 243
They Hunt to Eat, 243
Mountain Face, 244
Little Fishes, 244
Hope for Vultures, 245
Bodyguard, 245
Took a Look, 245
Rapper Gunned Down at Upscale Mall, 246
Mandatory Evacuation at 3 a.m., 247
Quake, 247
Pinkelponkers, 248
Short Takes of Marlon Brando, 249
Holy Family, 250
Sandwich, 250
A Pack Forms, 251
Bob Hope Lives Here, 251
Freeway, 252
Caminito Bravura, 252
Coyote, 253
The Bride, 253
Target Onshore, 254

9

La Jungla, 255
Lone Swimmer, 256
A Walk Near Guatemala, 257
The Lost Footsteps of Col. Fawcett, 258
Rio, 258

Midtown Ecology

1

BRYANT PARK

Piston backfires
a car on 42nd Street
and the pigeons lift in a flock
        and wheel away
in ancestral fear of gunfire
although these New York City birds
have never had to dodge the gun.

        When shots are real
the barrel is not aimed at them.

WOMAN SPEAKING ON BUS

Now anytime I want to visit him
I just take the Eighth Avenue subway.
It takes only twenty minutes or so,
        twenty or thirty,
and right where I come up the subway steps
        there's a little gate
and there he is, under a lovely tree.

                MOTH

If the moth with things on its antennae
        to jam bat-radar ultrasonic cries
            had offensive weapons too

    instead of being pinned through the middle
                in a specimen case
    that moth might be the national bird today

LATE AFTERNOON

Air bubbles burst in the aquarium,
an electric pump, a miniature,
hums in the background.
She is breathing deeply in her sleep.

Her mouth hangs open and her eyes are closed.
I'll let her rest on the couch, without disturbing
the nonchalant pose
in which pleasure surprised her.

AFTERNOON, CENTRAL PARK

the	and	because
senorita	talks	it
feeds	to	is
nuts	it	a
to	in	norte
a	broken	americano
squirrel	English	squirrel

BELLS

The cast-iron sounds bounce down from a Gothic belfry
with that extra bang stone can give to the sound of bells

into the cobblestone square, you might think,
of a town in France on Sunday morning —

but this is Oakland, New Jersey:
the bells sound from a small wooden
building topped by a cupola.

Standing near my car in the supermarket parking lot,
I lift up my eyes and I permit my heart to rejoice:
electronic stereophonic medieval bells.

DEAL

An old woman
opens the door
of the church

of the Immaculate Conception

and steps out
on 14th Street.

Her Mediterranean peasant
face is cracked in gratification.

Back in the church
she had struck
a hard bargain.

NOCTURNE, FROM A WINDOW

He opened the yellow Dodge
back door.

She slid in
and he leaned after her.

Kissed goodnight.

Then he withdrew,
closed the taxi door.

And left,
never looked back.

So?

Hard to say,
the way he walked away.

YOUR RIGHT NIPPLE

Your right nipple
reminds
me of the uppermost tip
of a state capitol dome

but your left nipple's different
your left nipple
reminds
me of other nipples

your lips
are the color
of a Macedonian sunset

CENTRAL PARK, EARLY MARCH

A kind woman sprinkles corn for the helicopters,
they're hungry, you can hear their bones rattle in the air,
the chill air — that pierces you through and through, pierces you
to the very bone. The woman kicks at a squirrel.
The rattling bones of helicopters become louder.

ROOFTOP LULLABY

The clouds tiptoe across the afternoon
above a brownstone and an empty lot

a hanging curtain of reflecting glass
that catches them a moment as they pass

the sun skids round a bend on tar and slate
the ventilator pipes begin to spin

no falcon silhouette against the blue
there's nothing in the sky to bother you

GULLS

The East River drains backward with the tide
and here and there a gull wheels, to circle,
dip and hover, investigate a thing
floating submerged in the green dock water,
paper undulating a limb whitely.

Do daddy seagulls eat dead people? No,
little girl, did your mother tell you that?
I suppose not, you thought of it yourself.

Daddy seagulls laugh, they are big and strong,
ah, you can almost smell the ocean breeze
waft in as fresh as aftershave lotion.

A NAME

A small tanker, the *Mary A. Whalen*,
rides high and empty out of the water,
steaming downriver, her red sides peeling.

Who is Mary A.? The captain's mother?

Mary, the shipowner's secretary?
(He's named a supertanker for his wife.)

Whalen? A good Irish name, to be sure.
A nurse perhaps who stood for no nonsense,
a sailor's friend through clap or high fever,
salty Nightingale, all-weather woman.

To call an oil tanker merely *Mary*
without last name or middle initial
dismisses the woman with a lyric,
ideal painted over the real —
the rusty work ships named for a goddess,
nymph, nun, infanta, dowager empress.

INTERRUPTED BY DAWN

But soft, what light through yonder window breaks?

It is the East. Had we but wings to fly
we could scorn the danger and tarry here,
you and I, wild in love's sweet abandon.

It's a working day, middle of the week,
soon the clock will ring and the bed will creak,
in less than an hour he will be awake.

While he heats the coffee upon the stove,
runs, slaps and tries to figure where in hell
are all these baby roaches coming from,
we'll nestle beneath the linoleum.

WASP

Sun came through the fifteen panes
        of air-clear glass
in an old-fashioned window.

A wasp inside was buzzing
        against the glass.

Had it been a butterfly
        I could have caught
and released it out of doors.

But black and yellow banded
        insects can sting.

Gauze calipers could have held
        the panicked beast
without damaging its wings.

Salvation is not sure for
        a thing that looks
like it has power to sting.

THE LADY IN THE LAKE

A car parked under a flowering tree
with a Japanese lake in its windshield.

The driver's face shimmers from deep beneath,
her frightened countenance swims in my gaze.

I reach my hand to her. The engine starts.

A VISITOR?

Although the shower curtains are getting old
the wings of the butterflies have not faded
in their mock hygienic shades of green and blue
among white flowers on translucent plastic
that's nearly rigid, perished by steam and age.

The midnight oil flickers in a naked bulb
on a cord from the ceiling, a bright bathroom,
sanctuary for thought and meditation.

The butterflies waver as a curtain moves
and no doubt because I am alone my heart
skips a beat and I wonder is there something
there behind that curtain or is it only
dry arthritic folds of plastic subsiding.

A phenomenon of polymer science?

Or has a dear departed former tenant
returned to his or her beloved shower?

One of the curtains is really moving –
it could be plastic readjusting itself
but the movement seems overelaborate,
a slow billowing and a quick contraction
with much deliberate rippling and curling,
folds crackling, curtains scraping against the tub.

I wait in silence for them to draw apart ...

IN A MIDTOWN POST OFFICE

He writes an airmail letter.

He is thin and very pale
and his clothes are worn but clean.

He finishes the letter.

His face is bland, it tells me
nothing, not a single thing.

An impersonal letter,
one that gives nothing away?

And back in the Old Country
do they remember him still?

The one who went to America ...

2

SUNDAY EVENING, JULY

A wind turns the paler underside of leaves,
the trees shimmer in waves of moving facets.

      The weekend crowd
load bicycles on cars to drive back to the city.

A watching girl about ten tells them she has never
      been to New York.

      Her father is
an army strongman, a tough balding paratrooper

who lives nearby, proud to be free of the contagion
      of urban blight,

      a hive alive
with scrapers, shredders, collectors and detritivores,

he has told me gravely over scotch and beer chaser
      in a tavern.

      But his daughter
watches them loading their shining ten-speed bicycles

and her expression is one of determination
      mixed with envy.

      She too would own
a French racing bicycle if only *she* lived there.

She is blonde, already pretty, unafraid to speak
      to the people

      from Manhattan,
so far from her hometown bumblebee economy.

EARLY LUNCH

This was when I worked in publishing,
twenty-somethingth floor, Sixth Avenue,
Rockefeller Center, tall buildings
shoulder to shoulder. I worked in
one of many identical
cubicles on one of many
identical floors, business suit, tie,
daily expecting to be replaced.

One early lunch I had too much
whiskey in Hurley's convenient bar
on an empty stomach, didn't eat,
came back to my desk to look at the Times
job ads and geopolitical scene,
only to find I was too late —
the revolution had taken place,
I was overthrown, dispossessed,
some upstart had taken my job,
had lost no time in putting his things
on the shelves in my office, my desk:
pens, folders, neat stacks of documents,
a framed photo of wife and children.

What had happened to my wilderness
of manuscripts and unanswered mail?

I stripped charts from walls, emptied desk drawers,
heaved out a locked-tight metal box,
ran the chair at high speed on its wheels
against a glass-topped steel partition.

Then I paused and had second thoughts
about the mess I had inflicted
on my employers for their deceit.
Strangers gathered but kept their distance.

That moment I looked through the window,
same floor of the building next door,
saw a man in shirtsleeves whom I knew,
knew him well because I worked with him.

Likely they had called security
by now: nightsticks, uniforms, handcuffs.

I made for the elevators,
the office workers backed away —
this wrecker was not a bum, he was
a haywire image of themselves.

No one stopped me in the lobby.

I crossed to the block in which I worked,
the look-alike building to the south.

Do you have enemies? A question
they must have asked the occupant
when he returned from lunch. Owe loan sharks?

Sorry for the inconvenience caused.

I blame the glass-box architecture.

ON A FLIGHT OF STEPS

I have nothing against anyone who
wants to sleep off wine or dope in the sun.
New built monoliths on the west side of
the Avenue of the Americas
provided hard but sun-warmed surfaces.
A flight of gentle steps, all extra wide,
carried a heavy load of passengers.
They seemed to be rolling from step to step.
I climbed around or over their bodies
and controlled an urge to kick some of them.

Later two women friends came to my desk.
They had been amazed to see me perform
with Trisha Brown (could have been someone else)
and they thought that I was one of the best
of the unsuspecting men in dark suits
climbing the steps through the modern dancers.

TAKEOVER

Shortly after California aeronautics flopped
Melvin, middle-aged, had to stoop to an editing job
and goad the company chess men in his first week at work.

I welcomed something new when I overheard his shrill
phone conversations with employee chess club members –
he told them he had watched them play and they weren't in his class.

I was bored out of my mind in the cubicle next to his
and I enjoyed the loud phone talk that burned up his working day.

Melvin took to calling various management levels
to pressure executives clutched high on the career ladder
to send him progress reports, which unquestioningly they did.

Some workers, half as old as Melvin, avoided him as weird –
everyone refused to sign the document he brought around.

The proclamation was grandiose, its wording notified
chairman, executive officers and board of directors
that herewith the employees had assumed company control.

Melvin entered a directors' meeting, announced the coup,
spelled out his terms for their continuing association
with the company under its employee leadership.

He held them chairbound for an hour, until one looked and found no
enraged employees slavering for blood outside the door.

No one hurt him. They escorted him from corporate quarters,
took security photographs, released him in the street,
told him not to come back, they'd forward his things and his pay.

That night Melvin broke a row of store windows somewhere in Queens.

BANK OF ELEVATORS

I press the down button, it lights beneath my finger.

The elevator doors slide open, it is empty.

Another pair of doors opens its metal petals
(something wrong with the computer?) and then another.

All three elevators wait, humming, clean, bright, empty.

Now the first doors move along their grooves, meet together,
then the second, the third, I hear sounds going away.

The light winks out within the elevator button.

HEAT, VISTAS, THE SOURCE, PACIFIC

A Mack truck, another load of frozen food,
        beating the red lights,
thunders by outside the window.

You cause my iron world reality
        to crash and burn,
throw me from the wreck I make of life

and keep me coming back for more
        of your sweet body.

ROOFTOP

Red legs and black toenails,
the pigeon struts and pouts,
hackles iridescent
pinks, greens, runs a circle
around his mate, bows, coos,
prepares to mount her back
to push against her in
wing-flapping ecstasy.

But she does not present
a submissive posture;
instead, walks off the roof
on a telephone line.

Despite virile ardor,
he finds this to be too
much a balancing act.

JONES BEACH, SEPTEMBER

Gulls stand on the uppermost reaches,
water flooding over webbed feet,
then ebbing over cheeks of sand.

The sun in murk a color spot,
a peculiar shade of red,
the beams are filtered by the smoke,
forest fires in Yellowstone park.

Carlos Santana plays guitar,
empty band shell, adjusting sound,
his concert starts at eight tonight.

Fathead jumbos circle offshore,
inbound delay at JFK.

Never seen the sea so calm before.

BUS STOP, JANUARY

Earmuffs, scarfs and thermal gear,
people wait, the bus stops here.

One shivers and others stamp,
they glance sideways at the vamp.

Her short skirt and her long legs,
she's not one of weather's dregs.

111 MOTT STREET

Chinese waiters, polite, smiling,
wait for the last eaters to leave.

Tsingtao. Tsingtao.

On a table, they place two chairs,
one upended on the other,
an ideogram: say farewell.

Tsingtao. Tsingtao.

BAG IN TREE

A white plastic bag
caught in a tree
(a gnarled sycamore's
witch-fingered twigs)
inflates and flaps
and sags, a wind-puffed
aerial condom

FRONTIER LIFE

I knew the color reproduction well
from books and magazines: a fur trader
dips a paddle in the smooth Missouri
from the stern of a dugout. Hides are piled
amid the craft. An Indian maiden
leans on them. Atop the prow, a black cat
with upright ears reflects in the water.

It always struck me as a touching show
of domesticity in wilderness,
Fur Traders Descending the Missouri,
George Caleb Bingham, 1845.

Exploring the real painting, I saw
two of my perceptions were mistaken:
the person leaning on the hides is not
a maiden but a young Indian man;
the cat silhouette contains a bear cub.

NEW YORK CITY, 1904

The Flatiron building's northern edge
looms like the prow of a giant ship
out of an early blue-green photo.

This technological icebreaker
noses aside the lamppost gaslight's
wavery reflections on wet streets.

3

MIDTOWN ECOLOGY

A peregrine
        diving down the glass-walled offices

hunts pigeons
        fattened on corn kernels by old women

on park benches
        from plastic bags manufactured by

their offspring
        with no time to peer out office windows

SHE THINKS BACK

When McCarthy went on witch hunts
in the fifties, room dark, she saw
lantern slides of known communists
and she could not believe her eyes,
she raised her hand, stood up and said,
"Miss, that one's my Uncle Harry."
Kids shouted and threw books at her.

Years later she recalled her shame.
On a visit her mother said,
"If you, as a young girl, were marked,
then think what things were like for me."
"For you?" "I was a communist."

NEAR RHINEBECK

You'd think with all the trees they'd perch in them
        birds on a wire
unless they're urban birds unused to trees
          north for the day
on tour like us to view the autumn leaves

Artery-red corpse-yellow blotched with plague
        perched in the trees
a million faces peeping back at us
          souls of the damned
ready to tear loose when the next wind screams

PHOTOS FROM SPACE

The Hubble space telescope
beamed back photographs of them.

Eggshell blue and blossom pink
interstellar gas and dust.

Some of them appear to have
gargoyle heads and pointed ears.

And nothing more? Among them
shines a pointy Christmas star.

Its pulse signals from the void,
anchored to no Bethlehem.

UNSEEN PASSENGER

I shiver in the night air
and belligerent peer in
a taxicab back window
at a fussy man
who searches for his wallet
and selects a note
to pay his fare, who then counts
his change carefully,
calculates a tip
and puts away his money,
gathers all his packages,
looks around him to make sure
he's leaving nothing.

With apologetic smile
he holds the cab door open,
shuts it after me.

The taxi rolls on
slowly toward a red light.
I give my destination.
The driver steps on the brake.

A French name on his license.
From his head and neck, I see
he's black, skinny, fortyish.
Probably Haitian.

How did you get in my cab?
he asks. His voice is trembling.
He turns his head then
slow and peers at me
and his eyes, they look frightened.

I think he knows that
sometimes a zombie
wears a round, pink Irish face.

SIGNALS

The school for special children
opens its summer doors
to extra special children

down the block from where I live
and this July the playground
invisible to me

is auditorium
to adolescent male
continual distinctive whoops

repetitive as hiccups
mellifluously remote
off center

out of sync
with other children's voices
a hermit's song to earth

a lone voice on its lone journey
I heard a year ago
and hear again today

a vocal equivalent
of gamboling robot
electronic beeps

the whoops have urgency
yet sound reflexive
a method of location

calling to mind
the navigational honks
of geese on a star-filled night

a formation invisible
wingtip to wingtip
in migratory flight

NUDE

Her body lying back
damp with sweat
not hers, mine

and on her perfect breasts
some chest hairs
not hers, mine

CHRISTMAS ON THIRD AVENUE

You might have wanted, Christmas Day,
to twist and crack the air
in the avenue and cross streets
like ice cubes in a tray.

A couple outside a liquor store —
its security gate down and locked —
bleary-eyed and well advanced in years,
she glared at him and he said to her,
Of course I knew that it was Christmas,
what I didn't know, it was today.

TAPEWORM

After the Texas oilman B.L. Bourke
had expelled a whitish length of tapeworm
in a hospital suite the doctor said,
regardless of length, he would not be rid
of the parasite till they saw its head.

Next day, once more, B.L.'s bowels were purged
and yet another whitish length emerged,
again without the all-important head.

The doctor saw the gun beside the bed.

B.L. claimed he knew what he had to do:
Soon as this critter showed its goddam head,
put a slug between its eyes — kill it dead.

RAMADAN

I asked the taxi driver named Mahomet
if cool weather in New York had made it harder
to fast during Ramadan. He said, no,
it made it easier — it took your mind off
your emotions. In the Sudan, he remembered,
when the sun was directly overhead,
moving the bolts in the corrugated roof,
and you could drink no water yet for many hours,
that was where you knew God was talking to his people.

ARK

It starts innocuously ...
a spotted rabbit perhaps,
then cats of several kinds,
a turtle, a frog, a seal
and a crystal elephant.

It builds insidiously ...
ewes and lambs, a shepherdess,
collie dogs, a leprechaun,
a harp, a zebra, dolphins,
giraffe families, a goat.

Beasts continue to gather
and they stand in little herds
on sideboards of cherrywood,
windowsills, the mantelpiece,
tabletops and walnut shelves.

A ginger kitten, white bib
and feet, only three months old,
claws sliding on the polish,
breaks a few china creatures,
pieces the grandnieces hide.

MOURNING DOVE

The mourning dove
starts up his tune
before first light.

We hope he meets
a nice bird soon.

And when he does
we can expect
to hear him croon.

MESSAGE RECEIVED

Speaking of how people can be inclined
to take the things you say literally,
remember your friend who wanted a child
but could not conceive, even after she
had tried just about everything that she
could think of and then decided that she
should have herself checked out medically,
her husband also, and was found to be,
the pair, capable of procreation?

You explained about bicycling motion —
to think of her legs pushing on pedals —
to open her womb for seed to be sown
once her avid husband's climax was done.

She phoned to say you should get a medal —
your advice had worked beyond all belief,
she was three months gone, and what a relief
not to have to, anymore, leave warm sheets
and cycle madly up and down the streets.

A WARM EVENING

Honeybees nuzzled the blossoms
            printed on her dress
and made her shriek and lift her hair.

At a wooden picnic table
            under maple leaves
she tongued the ice cubes in her drink.

An hour later I heard her laugh
            at something the men
had joked about who sat with her

before a row of clear plastic
            inverted glasses,
each with a loud imprisoned bee.

A VISITOR BY NIGHT

a bumblebee
the size of a golf ball
droning like a World War II
superfortress but losing altitude when hit by tissue paper flak
hymenopteran dead reckoning
navigation
shot to shit
now
the dark

a light bulb

THIEF

I was a thief
and you had
power over me
and sent me to a place
where there was nothing to steal
and I stayed there
without stealing —
did that make me
more virtuous?

No, you deprived me
of moral choice —
I had no
opportunity to be
less virtuous.

A second question:
if you made me
no better,
did you make me
any worse?

Before you sent me away
I stole four times a week
but resisted
the temptation
eight times a week
and thereby exercised
some virtue.

By depriving me
of chances to steal
you stole from me
my virtue.

BOUQUET

On the arm of the groom
the bride in her white dress
came down from the altar
carrying white flowers.

You might have expected,
the woman said, roses
or some flower like that
but she embraced daisies.

Daisies would have been nice —
honest, simple and wild —
but as she came closer
I saw they were plastic.

THREE DIALOGUES

1
Ever kill anyone?

Two tours in Vietnam.

You killed people?

I killed people.

Do they ever come now
to you in dreams?

Yes, all the time.

What do they say?

I never know — they speak
Vietnamese.

That's a joke, right?

The joke's on me,
they tell me things
and I hear the lingo
but I never know
what they say to me.

2
You ever been
a crime victim?

I was hit on the head
with a hammer
by a serial killer.

Did they catch him?

No.

Did you know him?

No. He was a stranger
who saw me on the street
and hit me for no cause.

How do you know
he's a serial killer?

You can't go round
hitting women on the head
with a hammer
without killing some of them.

How do you know
he goes around
hitting women on the head
with a hammer?

Because that's what
he did to me.

3
Those roses are frozen.
When you bring them inside
their petals will open
and fall.

And how long will that take?

Four hours.

I'll have plenty of time.

LINDEN

The small linden tree
hardly ten feet tall
has overdone it

sprouting blossoms in
quantities greater
than look natural

like a teenage girl's
much too heavily
applied cosmetics

GRASS AND STUFF

It's frightening
in the suburbs:

all those kitchen windows
and behind each one
a poet looking out
philosophizing
about the backyard

TWITCH

Don't feel sorry for the girl
with neurological tics
opposite you
on the subway.

Beneath her hair, her earbuds
throb with music.

She is dancing.

OUT THERE

He had lived in the asylum
a long time exactly how long
he could not tell

He had newspapers and television
but somehow over time
he had lost touch

He had seen planes
orange flames of bursting bombs
people running and children

Television showed it happening
somewhere out there
where he might easily have been

Would he have curled up
in a cellar
with his thumb in his mouth

Or would he have jumped
from wall to wall
and danced among the flames

No one could predict
what he might do
out there in the real world

INTERRUPTED CALL

The man standing
talking on his cell phone
perhaps they thought he was speaking to them

the old pair
who had taken so long
to get off the bus and look around them

five feet tall
and both about ninety
the talking man never saw them coming.

The old man stood
close to the talking man
looked up and began to say things to him

while the woman
having caught her heel
in a grating had to clutch the arm

arm of the man
talking on the cell phone
who found it harder now to ignore them.

He pocketed
his little telephone
freed her heel and pointed their way to them

gazed after them
a moment bewildered
then smiled at a thought and reached for his phone.

A LANDMARK GONE

She discovered that her high school had been razed and in its place
squatted a multistory office block whose rows of windows
        glistened like scales.

I told her of a friend, daughter of a Kansas wheat farmer,
        whose family,
on sultry nights when the radio or television called
a tornado alert, slept in a cinderblock storm cellar
        beneath the house
and who emerged one sunny morning and found no house, only
        empty prairie.

She claimed she could accept the work of God or mother nature
        or whatever
more readily than greed of some property developer.

LAST WISH

Put my ashes in the river
that flows back and forth with the tide.

Up and down I'll wander
on Manhattan's East Side.

A SIGHT TO SEE

It takes a lot to draw a crowd
        to peer inside
        a store window
along Lexington Avenue.

Seven Abyssinian cats
        extend their necks
        and gaze as if
they lay along the ancient Nile.

Two blocks south I meet a painter
        and though I think
        his work abstract
I say to him they're worth a look.

He has no use for people who
        love animals
        and hate children,
he shouts and walks away from me.

It might help relieve his anger
        for him to spend
        a little time
curled up with cats in a basket.

HALLOWEEN

Don't assume in the West Village
that all the tall physically fit
women with brightly tinted hair
are drag queens. In this day and age
they could be tall physically fit
women with brightly tinted hair.

GET YOURSELF A DOG

The chihuahua stands fiercely on his toes
on the padded seat of an empty wheelchair,
          waiting anxiously.

Through its window, he tries to see inside the store.
Touch that chair and he'll tear you to pieces.
          Or thinks he will.

Gripping a cane in a malformed hand,
an elderly woman limps out of the store
          and calls to him.

Eyes popping, yipping nonstop, all four
legs stiffened, the little dog vibrates
          in excitement.

It brings to mind the sardonic advice:
if you want unconditional love —
          what you need to get.

ILL WIND

A shade flapped and pushed it from the sill,
it hit the carpet and didn't break,
and though I claimed it was hideous
and I'd hide it after you were gone,
I never did. Now an ill wind brings
the thought something has happened to you.

4

HOSPITAL FLOOR

Shrink the huge corridor
to Ancient Roman length,
its linoleum tiles
will become mosaic.

No Venus, Ganymede,
Neptune, goat or dolphin
cavorts across the beige
expanse this floor presents.

VIEW

You are the kind of person who notices
      the bluish silvery gray
        of river, buildings and sky
          or you are not

But do not underestimate people who
      need to have things pointed out
      before the perception strikes
        and we can see

INDEPENDENCE DAY ON THE HUDSON RIVER

The uppermost oak planks
of an abandoned pier
are bleached and weathered to
their spinal elements,
eaten by sun and wind
into brown dragon shapes.

We crowd the riverbank
to view tall-masted ships
parade the water in full sail.

This shore was clogged with sailing craft
when these top planks were newly nailed
upon the pier, the wind was fresh,
the sun was comatose
and horseless carriages were cheered.

WARNING GEESE

Seven Canada geese
twitch their heads and white chins
and rest their heavy bosoms

on the Middle School lawn
in the shade of a tree
in Westport, Connecticut,

demonstrating perhaps
in their anserine way
the risks of education

ME AND THE MOB

After all this time
it's probably safe
now to confess.

I am the one
who sideswiped
the Cadillac

at 2 a.m.
outside the social club
on Mulberry Street.

It was double parked
and I sped away,
expecting bullets.

In time we learned
the FBI
had bugged the club —

they played the tapes
to nail the wiseguys
on conspiracy charges.

I want the court to know
that metal scrape you heard
was made by me.

STYLE

Buy New York boutique socks
knitted by blind children
prisoners of Third World war

Socks organic in color
yellow for the desert
black for the jungle night
barefoot for evening wear

WOMAN WITH A QUESTION

She looked up and saw her mother
sit on the windowsill,
three flights above the ground.

She remembered her mother called,
sitting on the windowsill:
Why do you hardly ever
come to visit me,
you or your sister?

Next thing was, she saw her mother
push away from the window
and sail downward through the air.

She must have closed her eyes.

She heard the sound of her mother
hit the ground beside her.

She looked in the blue eyes
of the handsome detective
who brought her a cup of tea.

Had it occurred to her,
he needed to know
though he didn't like to ask,
her mother tried to kill her?

She looked in those blue eyes
and saw cold laughter dancing there.

Had her mother tried to kill her?

She never told her sister.

Instead she discussed it
with men she met in bars
who listened attentively
to what she had to say.

She then asked their opinion.

Their eyes almost always
gave their thoughts away:

What kind of woman —
they were usually thinking —
would tell this kind of story
to some guy she had only
just met in a bar?

GOETHE HOUSE RECITAL

Mozart is known to have visited the house
while this clavichord was there, he said, wringing
his hands, so it's reasonable to assume,
I think, his immortal fingers touched those keys.

The furniture mover didn't seem to hear.
A large man in jeans, check shirt and biker boots,
he reassembled the early piano,
watched by anxiety clad in a gray suit.

My God, this instrument was imported whole
from Germany, he said. Yet, from Long Island,
you bring it here in pieces, a treasure not
taken apart in at least a hundred years.

The furniture mover was fetching a chair.
He sat at the keyboard, smiled and raised his hands.
He played. His nervous watcher kept his distance.
Ah, he said disapprovingly, Scarlatti.

ON THE SIDE OF A BUILDING

Uncovered, the painting on the bricks
is the height and width of the building,
not a scene with Venus or Bacchus —
after all, this is New York — a face,
a huge terra cotta colored face,
black eyebrows, black eyes and black mustache,
Mediterranean, Latino.

The paint on some bricks has paled or peeled,
creating a mosaic effect.
He must have meant something once to be
so big. Some archive may hold beliefs
associated with this image.
There they wait to be discovered
before his visage runs in rain or fades.

THREE STORM WARNINGS

You know a storm is on its way when
the red-breasted sawbill diving ducks
arrive from bay and open water,
when winds draw stretch marks on river skin,
when the television weather folk
dance in front of radar weather maps

BANNER AND DRUMS

The Columcille Pipe and Drum Band
piped and drummed, piped and drummed its way,
Fifth Avenue, St. Patrick's Day.

The pipers headed for the pubs
when the march was finally done,
welcome anywhere, with a drone

and bag of air, leaving drummers
with their drums. In front of a bar
I met a drummer with his snare.

He knew I lived not far away
and asked if he and a few friends
who had marched and drummed in the band

could use my place to dump their things.
Seeing their instrumental plight,
I said I'd keep stuff overnight:

      a banner on two gilt-tipped poles
      of Columcille in Kingdom Come,
      five snares and the band's large bass drum.

He never phoned to pick them up.
Weeks went by, and my wife complained
space was lost, and her patience waned.

I phoned. The drummer was amazed,
said he couldn't thank me enough
and asked me where I found their stuff.

Band members were having meetings
to try to trace each man's movements
and try to pinpoint the moment,

unbelievable as it seemed,
when all their gear, treated with care,
just disappeared into thin air:

      a banner on two gilt-tipped poles
      of Columcille in Kingdom Come,
      five snares and the band's large bass drum.

TAXI ON LEXINGTON

When she was very young,
the taxi driver says,
her parents wouldn't let
her cut her hair. It grew
so long when combed it came
to the back of her thighs.

They stand out in traffic,
cars in tomato red,
not harsh — a soft red,
a tomato shade.

Her father said she
couldn't cut it till
she married and asked
her husband's permission.

The taxi is lemon.

Her kayak team had
planned a competition.
The water was cold
and if you tumbled in
with long hair and no
hair dryers back then
in Romania you
could get pneumonia.

They let her cut her hair.

GOOD MORNING

The cat jumped across the air shaft,
        five stories up,
to land upon a pigeon
on the opposite window ledge.

        It sank canines
through puffed iridescent feathers
        to seize the bird
        by its scrawny neck.

Holding the pigeon in its jaws,
        wings beating feebly,
the cat leaped back and entered
        the open window.

It placed its gift still throbbing
        beside the head
sleeping on the pillowcase
and waited for the clock to ring.

UNIDENTIFIED SAINT

I can guess the identity
of many saints from their statues
but I didn't know the bearded
gentleman in robe and sandals.

From the statue's placement and its
colorful plaster and large size,
he was a saint to reckon with.

A woman walked the church's length
to touch his foot and talk to him —
and left him with a playful slap.

ONLY A WAVELENGTH AWAY

        I don't have cable TV
and lousy highrises block my reception

        I was interested to see
a homeless guy in a wheelchair late at night

        on the sidewalk his TV
hooked to the base of a streetlight clear picture

        got me thinking it could be
the metal streetlight made a good antenna

WESTWARD

Snow covered the imperfections
of Union City, New Jersey.

Bill and I sat in the front, Bill
at the wheel, taking the highway.

The two women sat in the back,
involved in their realities.

Ann said, I've seen that spire before,
we must be going in circles.

Leave the driving to me, Bill said,
and we continued our talking.

Minutes later she said, That spire
again! We're going in circles!

I acknowledged that the two spires
had certain similarities –

might even belong to churches
of the same religious belief.

When the spire did not move it raised
another possibility.

I opened my door and said, Bill,
try keeping your foot on the gas.

The rear wheels spun in soft inches
of snow. Its untouched surface blurred

an exit lane. The car belly
rested on a traffic island.

Spires of old were travelers' guides
as this one was this snowy day.

ON THE WAY UP

When I saw my office looking south on midtown
on the twenty-eighth floor of the glass-walled highrise
I said to myself I must be more important
in my new job than I had anticipated
to be assigned such a clearly high-status view.

Being more important than I had expected
made me feel like a more responsible member
of society and almost a major cog
in the corporate gears though I a newcomer
was still learning to find my way to the men's room.

In May it was warm in June warmer in July
it suddenly dawned on me that only someone
wearing swimming trunks could remain behind my desk
in mid afternoon with the air conditioning
arranged for office comfort on the cool north face.

A FERRARI

My Buick,
its V8 engine
goes full bore.

No silencer,
foot to floor
hear this baby roar.

Leaving town
I pass a clown
in a Ferrari.

He stabs a finger
at his dashboard,
meaning radar.

I slow down
and see ahead
a police car.

Drive by
a Ferrari
and ask why.

ENLARGED DETAIL

After Wayne Alan Russo
the names of Edward Ryan,
John Joseph Ryan, Jr.,
Jonathan Stephan Ryan,
Matthew Lancelot Ryan,
Tatiana Ryjova,
Christina Sunga Ryook —

medical examiner's
list of dead and missing in
the World Trade Center attack —

Ryans, Ryjova, Ryook,
the people who did nothing
worse than go to work that day

FIRST ANNIVERSARY
OF TWIN TOWERS

The sixteen acre hole in the ground
could be mistaken for a building site —
no atmosphere of disaster
distinct from the everyday kind
to which we are all accustomed.

A ten minute walk from where I live,
the sidewalk is wide outside a firehouse.
Nine died from there: eight men, one woman.
The sidewalk is almost blocked by flowers,
ornamental plants and small bushes
in vases, bottles, earthen pots and
foil-covered plastic containers,
a daisy in a paper cup,
wreaths on stands, piled against the building.

Passersby have to walk around
this immense quantity of vegetation.
Most stop, stalled by the impact of emotion.

WHY ARE YOU WALKING?

What were you doing?
All you were doing
was walking daily
without waiting for
the photographers
to finish viewing
their loved ones posing
before a background
United Nations.

That is why you are
in many photos
in side view striding
on your daily way,
oblivious to
the photographers,
about to appear
in their viewfinders
as they clicked the shot.

In Japan alone
your image appears
in many thousands
of photographers'
shots of their loved ones
posing before the
United Nations.
This is not confined
to Japan alone.

It can only be
a matter of time
before an army
supercomputer
detects a pattern
in your recurring
image at this site.
The photographers
will not protect you.

SHOWER

There's no soap or no shampoo
among the bottles and tubes,
some of which stand on their heads,
with names like Apricot Scrub
or single-word labels in
elegant calligraphy
implying unreadably
that they may not be for you,
but no soap or no shampoo

LIVE PERFORMANCE

She searches endlessly in a bag.
      The bag is plastic.
      The acoustics
of Carnegie Hall amplify its rustle.

The orchestra is playing a slow movement.
      A smaller bag
      within the larger bag
may contain the thing for which she searches.

The smaller bag is also plastic
      and it rustles
      as she tussles
to locate still smaller bags within.

In time the rustling grows on me
      sitting near her,
      not hearing water
while dwelling next to a mountain stream.

QUANDARY

How does a poet persuade
people to read his poems?

As Joseph Schumpeter said,
it's not enough to produce
a satisfactory soap,
it's also necessary
to induce people to wash.

IT CAN'T BE HERE

I wake to smell of burning
in my fifth-floor apartment
and am already rationalizing
(it may just be boiler fumes)
already altering reality
before wakeful perception.

        As sirens approach
it's hard to remain under my blanket
        despite bitter cold
        till I can decide
by keen listening now fully alert
at which house exactly the sirens die.

They're not outside my building
I am fairly sure of that —
besides there's no commotion
in stairwell or corridors —
unless of course everyone
is lying still like me and listening.

        Shattering of glass
and the sound of a door ripped from its frame
(one of the kicks of being a fireman)
        someone calling to
        a victim perhaps
collecting the family photographs.

OBITUARY

After his death she told his life story,
beginning with infant wails of distress
being answered quickly by his mother,
which caused him to develop a secure
attachment to her, trusting in her
availability, showing a lack
of fearfulness, as such infants do.

She guessed this from his tranquil marriage,
since infants with secure attachments
go on to enjoy unconflicted
adult intimate relationships.

His father, when home, liked to take him
to look out to sea in heavy weather.

A DRIVE IN THE COUNTRY

Ken Kadish, Reuben's son,
in his furniture-moving days told me
he moved a woman's things
from Staten Island to south Ohio.

She asked him to move her
to some little town out in the middle
of nowhere, he did not
ask why and without maps did not know where.

He felt like a lonesome
solitary drive deep in the country
but when he saw her stuff
he said it would cost her less to throw it

away and buy new things
than truck it a third of the way across
America. She said
everything she owned was coming with her.

The woman could have been
his mother and Ken was none too pleased when
she climbed inside the truck
beside him and said she was set to go.

Across New Jersey and
Pennsylvania and then Ohio
it became a long haul
all day and all night into a new dawn.

Ken asked about the town —
Yellowbud, Elm Grove, Mount Joy or Good Hope,
I don't recall its name —
and she said that she had never been there.

She said she liked the name
and that was why she was coming to live
and though he might not see
things the way she did, she would need his help

in locating a house
to rent and from his point of view somewhere
he could unload his truck
and be rid of her and her paradise.

FRANCOIS

The doctor refused the quail eggs and champagne
at the trendy, monied art show opening.
He said, It's hard to believe that yesterday
afternoon I was treating starving children
in Ethiopia, and now I'm afraid
if I drink I might start yelling at people.

ASK NOT

The bell is saying its metal words
just loud enough to be heard
over evening traffic

Its heavy sounds drag themselves
along East 47th Street
to the United Nations

Gently slowly they resonate
in mature resignation
as daylight is fading

The tones hang in the air
outside a Japanese museum
in the middle of the block

I think of peace and order
and discipline and zen
and tranquility

But this bell peals next door
from a Catholic church
and it tolls for me

GREENWOOD MEN

Blow up a photo
to six feet in height
and ten feet across,

if the focus holds
almost anything
becomes an eyeful.

In full color on
a gallery wall
trees and undergrowth

stand in leaf on fields
in which wheat is shorn.
It may be France or

northern Germany,
the hills are gentle
and the sky is blue.

The trees and bushes
are nothing special,
hardly worth a look.

But stare at the leaves
till they undeceive.
Tell me what you see.

Men in camouflage
stand in open view
in front of the trees,

holding the matte stocks
of assault rifles,
and look back at you.

Once you have seen them
you can't believe how
you could have missed them.

Their faces are like
the stone faces high
on cathedral walls.

I HATE TO SAY IT

I don't know you and I
hate to say it but
your before and after
head shot photographs
in the newspaper ad
have got me thinking
you looked much better
with your previous face
than with the childish look
the surgeon gave you

THINKING OF HOME

With smiles the exiles think of home
in ways they never thought of home
when they lived in the land called home.

Think like we think, be more like us,
adopted homeland people say,
why would you want to be like you?

We do not want to be like us,
we are not who you think we are,
our children will not be like us.

Before we left we were like you
but here we changed to meet the things
regardless you expect from us.

Longtime exiles think of a home
in words they never found for home
when they grew in a place called home.

5

SUBWAY PASSENGER

I notice him enter the subway car
and stand by the door with outer borough
truculence and blood dripping from one sleeve
of leather jacket. He follows my look
down to the pool of blood starting to form
by his right foot, bright arterial blood
dripping in big drops, enlarging the pool.
He stares ahead. A stab or gunshot wound
maybe. I don't do a thing. If he keeps
losing blood he will hit the deck before
the train enters the tunnel to Brooklyn,
several minutes after I get off.

ON THEIR WAY

Today in New York City
the person who just shoved you
is less likely to be some
overenergetic male
from the inner city than
a financial services
employee with a college
degree in making money.

In a South Tower photo
after the second plane hit
but before the building fell
you can see people who are
not cops or firemen shoving
their way inside against the
stream of survivors-to-be
fast exiting the building.

NOT THIS RELIC

You are advised to cut in four
your driver's license once expired
to prevent its fraudulent use.

I sneer in some collector's eyes
scanning a horde of obsolete
licenses and certificates,

finding my face and wondering
what it was like to be alive
back then. I cut the thing in four.

ENCOUNTER

Two middle-aged
men staggered out
a saloon door
mid afternoon.

One scrutinized
a kid pushed
in a stroller
by his mother.

Get on your feet
and walk, he yelled.

The kid looked big
to be pushed
in a stroller
by his mother.

Get up and walk,
the drunk shouted.

His rage level
made his buddy
smile at mother
and shake his head.

CROSSING A STREET

As I walked against the light
and the car approaching slowed,
I gratefully waved and crossed.

He accelerated, braked,
called me a number of things
without saying why, drove off.

He perceived what came to mind,
instead of a grateful wave
he saw me give the finger.

HUDSON RIVER SOLITAIRE, NEAR RHINECLIFF

This Hudson winter evening
the sun drops without any
nonsensical visual display.

The river cold is blowing
as I walk alone along
the eastern bank's railroad embankment.

A ribbon of swamp is trapped
between the embankment and
what may once have been the river bank.

No trains running and no birds
flying and no fish jumping,
it is lonely in the fading light.

But this is what suits my mood,
this bleakness and cold and what
it must be like to have solitude.

Imagine my surprise when
men with guns stand up in blinds
and shout at me to get out of there.

LABEL

She handed me a bottle of wine
and said her husband would pick her up
sometime after midnight. I'd never
met her before – she was someone's friend
and seemed to know several people,
who greeted her. I gave her a drink.

She had brown eyes, full lips and big hips.
The wine she brought was Chateau Lafite
and I hid it where it would not be
poured accidentally. She said she'd
grabbed a bottle of her husband's wine
as she rushed out, late as usual.

A big man with wide shoulders and gold
teeth, a broken nose, he seemed annoyed
I said to take his wine with him when
they left. At a Manhattan party
nights ago his bottle of Lafite
had been dumped in the sangria bowl.

COMFORT SHOPPING

Three young women in a restaurant,
all having separately walked home
from Midtown to the East Eighties
on day two of the transit strike:
Did you buy anything? one asked.

How could I pass a thousand stores
and not buy something? one replied.

The third seemed relieved and told them,
I thought I was the only one.

NO SIXPACK

Are you off the brew?

The beer was never
for me – it was for
himself. He passed on.

Oh, he said, that's sad.

My bag is lighter
now he's gone, she said,
just reminding me.

Again he said, Sad.

It is, she agreed.

OUTSIDE A BUILDING

A white woman screamed.
A black man stood next
to her. We all looked
at him, as she kept
screaming. He pointed
to some bins. A mouse,
he said, nervously.

A DETAIL FROM REALITY

You can learn from TV shows like *Cops*
stuff you might easily overlook
or miss entirely in daily life,
for example, the tattooed guy who
called after shooting a tattooed friend
in what the guy claimed was self-defense.

Beside the body, on the tile floor,
lay a pizza slice, missing a bite –
found still clenched between the corpse's teeth.

Who would attack, an officer asked,
while biting on a slice of pizza?

WAITING TO CROSS THE STREET

A child in a stroller howled in rage
while her aggravated mother looked
another way and would not concede.

A young man in a business suit
looked at the child and urgently spoke
on his cell phone, perhaps explaining
to the beautiful woman he loved

that these were not the screams of a child
being slowly crushed by a truck's wheel
and that he was not standing aside
to avoid her blood on his new shoes.

JOKE AS POEM

You probably have heard this already:
the girl who is late for a concert asks
where Carnegie Hall is located and
nobody knows. She sees a man climbing
the subway steps with a violin case.
He will know. Please tell me, she asks, how do
I get to Carnegie Hall? Sadly he
whispers to her, Practice, practice, practice.

THE DARK SIDE

In his veins, egrets lift from the black
glistening mangrove roots. Iguanas
move their heads to look and caimans ease
beneath the liquid top, nostrils, eyes.

A disposable syringe dangles
by its needle from his upper arm.

He balances the wobbling canoe.

WHAT CAN WE DO?

Easy to say that she knows no other
kind of life, probably feels no deeper
pain as hope for change recedes with greater
age, she never could be called a weeper,
always proves herself to be a keeper
of commitments, concedes that she can err,
oh what in the world can we do for her?

SUBWAY FOAM

You can come home from work and get
major sleep and then head out
for activities prolonged
into the early hours
of the following day
and show up for work on time.

This was what he was doing when
he overdid the alcohol
and during a stop at home
to quench his continuing thirst
he ate a couple of quarts
of strawberry ice cream.

On the subway to work he
had a gastric attack
in a crowded passenger car
and blew pink bubbles from his mouth
like a diver under water
releasing bursts of oxygen.

He remembered how people
emptied the car around him
as he regurgitated streams
of pearlescent popping bubbles
a powerful memory
the nausea of strawberry.

CAWK SPOKE SQUAWK

Two Asian women talking very loudly
on the bus were interrupted by a male
Cawk who spoke their language. Seemingly upset,
they soon got off. What were you saying to them?
his wife asked. I never heard anyone here
speak Squawk before – it's not what I said, he said,
but the fact that someone here could understand
what they were saying. I might have made them lose
their sense of privacy in America.

A GOD OFFENDED

Out of nowhere lightning strikes
a late-model family car
on Lexington Avenue
going slow in the center lane.

An eccentric javelin
of flame hits the car's steel roof
and jumps a moment later
to a steel manhole cover
the car has just passed over,
hitting with a loud report.

The car stops, its hazard lights
are blinking, its driver
emerges cautiously,
waves traffic by in other lanes
and looks at the wheels and paintwork,
puzzled and unaware of this
bolt from the quiver of Zeus,
sky god, lord of the wind, clouds, rain
and thunder, omnipresent,
omniscient and omnipotent.

You can smell ozone in the air.

STAR TREK ENCOUNTER

First my daughter and then my son,
seven and nine at the time,
in the park near the mayor's
official residence,
stopped and stared at a man.

At the iron rail
high above the draining tide
stood the first officer
of the starship *Enterprise*.

Without a trace of a smile
Spock looked at my children,
held up his right hand
in the Vulcan salute and said,
Live long and prosper.

This was years ago and even then
Leonard Nimoy must have had enough
of Mr. Spock, yet he behaved
with dignity

as a representative
of the planet Vulcan
and with the decorum expected
of a Starfleet officer.

We walked some way before
my children managed a word.

WEAVING CAR

The car ahead is weaving
over the nearly empty
eastbound concrete expanse of

the Cross-County Expressway.
Giving the car a wide berth
I accelerate past and

watch in the rearview mirror.
The car creeps up to pass me
and I let it go because

I'm driving with my children.
As the car passes I see
it is packed with teenage guys.

Ahead once more the car slows
and moves to block me and then
moves aside to let me pass.

Out a back window a guy
aims a revolver but sees
my kids next to me and hauls

the snubnose gun back inside.
I know he has a mother
who some day in tears may tell

the media reporters
that to her he was always
a good boy and loving son.

SINGING WOMAN

She has an awful voice she says
and after only a few sips
of alcohol she gets an urge
to sing and then she cannot stop.

Her friends all say don't offer her
a drink or you will see that she
can drive you crazy and us too
although we like to hear her talk.

Streets and Avenues

1

A PIANIST'S DEPARTURE

Some say they favor the hit-or-miss
style of Arthur Rubinstein over
the manicured manipulations
of the great Vladimir Horowitz,

not on my mind as I walked in the
nineties between Park and Lexington
in the very early morning hours
when people asked me to be quiet

since Mr. Horowitz was dying –
gentle vigilantes who appealed
to all that was kind and good in me
to let the great man expire in peace.

It seemed then a misunderstanding
that he might prefer to shuffle off
his mortal coil in total silence
than hear distant singing in the street.

INWARD EYE

A psychiatrist told me women thought
he could look into their innermost depths
when he knew with little more than a glance
how their lives had gone since he saw them last.

All he did was look at her hair and know
when a woman felt good about herself.

CONJUROR

Flash the six of hearts and seven of diamonds
and quickly place these two cards face down on top

of the pack you placed face down on the table.
Use power of mind to cause these two cards to

migrate downward by magic to the bottom
of the pack. Then pick up the pack of cards and

flash the six of diamonds and seven of hearts
previously placed by you on the bottom.

Shuffle the cards and do not repeat the trick
and note how many believe and few observe.

MIGRATING BUTTERFLY

A monarch butterfly flapped inside
the glass door of TD Bank. He held
the door open so that it escaped
outside and resumed its journey south.

A woman just then exiting the bank
was touched by his humanity and smiled
at him. He said a lot of butterflies
visit this New York bank on their journey
south and visit next the Miami branch.

Alarm flickered in her eyes, alarm
on letting down her guard a moment
with an unknown man and seeing him
change from touchingly kind to plain weird
in a moment, over butterflies.

SUPERMARKET INCIDENT

Their green skulls freshened by time-controlled mist,
boston, romaine and iceberg smile at me
in rows. I select a head and I shake
water from its drenched leaves. A woman screams.

MEMORIAL AT FIRST AND 49TH

A ghost bicycle sprayed white is chained
to a street lamp in memoriam.
Cardboard tells her name but only says
hit by a car not whether it was
a hit and run. I think of her not
as one of those heavy brutes who ride
helmeted and knee padded and who
speed with homicidal negligence
among the elderly and infants
unprotected and unexpecting.
I think she wobbled in a long skirt
and was laughing on her telephone.

PATIENT BREAK

The old guy already had two thirds
of his body inside the saloon,
clutching the door protectively to
his chest as he talked to a woman
outside, much younger, a caregiver.
You can't come in – you would lose your job,
he said, take a walk around the block.
It's raining, she said. I won't be long,
he promised. She muttered unamused
in her language things known about men.

COUPLES

1
You look like one of those,
he said, pink wild roses.

She sniffled and replied,
I feel more like ragweed.

2
Looking in a diamond dealer's window,
we see a hundred chips of what might be
very expensive disappointing glass.

When we turn to go, an angle of light
hits with the optics of a welder's torch.

3
She asked, Did you see her shoes?

He asked, Did I see her shoes?

I saw you looking at her –
surely you noticed her shoes.

I didn't look at her shoes.

4
I think
I'll make
carrot soup,
she said.

Where will you
find them?
he asked.

Find what?

The parrots.

5
Please don't make me laugh,
she said. I feel like
staying mad at you.

6
Just when she
got all her
movie posters hung
the way she wanted
them he

TELEPHONES

1
A woman chatting on her telephone
while standing in a supermarket aisle
holding row upon row of cans of beans
unthinkingly reaches to rearrange
some of them so their labels now face out

2
I'll say no more about women
talking on mobile telephones
now I've seen a man with a phone
stand at a urinal and piss
and not miss a word of his call

A LESSON IN PRICING

It was all for charity so
he set a price of five dollars
for every book on the table
but did not sell one in two hours.

The director of marketing
thought it a hoot he was a goof:
she upped the prices, then slashed them,
most from thirty dollars to ten.

He sold nearly all of the books
within an hour despite the fact
they were now double the price
of what they had been before.

GENERATIONS

She, her daughter grown,
chats while grandson roams
in grandmother's home.

This feels good, he says.
His small hand squeezes
a breast prosthesis.

Grandma says in fun,
This shows his tastes run
in our direction.

IN A CROSSTOWN BUS

"I don't want to speak to you – let me speak to Josephine,"
                she says on her telephone.
        Someone behind loudly masticates
                crackly junk food.
        The bus waits as a truck blocks the lane.

"If I wanted to speak to you, I would have asked for you –
                let me speak to Josephine."
        Someone behind is tearing a new
                crinkly package.
        The driver stops for wheelchair access.

"I said I won't speak to you – let me speak to Josephine."

IN BROOKLYN

An old guy walks the local market aisles,
consulting a list and choosing items.

Other old guys play golf or walk the beach –
he likes to shop for food his wife will cook.

Two thugs shadow him. They keep their distance
and keep an eye on him and on the door.

Finished, he wheels his cart to the cashier,
a young guy who's all mouth and attitude.

This guy likes to show he does not respect
the old guy with his list and shopping cart.

The thugs know the look on the old guy's face
when he means that they should keep out of things.

Eventually the young guy hears about
who it is he has been disrespecting.

My God, he thinks, the Godfather did not
have them break my legs, and now he is quick

to greet the old guy with the cart and say,
Yes, sir, no problem, Mr. Gambino.

One day the old guy looks at him and says,
You were better the way you were before.

BY THE WAYSIDE

I stepped over them every sunny afternoon
       as they rested weary selves
             on warm concrete.

Where are they now? Gone, like the snows of yesteryear.
       The city fathers found them
          resting places

          I know not where –
but where supine forms will not diminish the price
       of property per square foot.

       Yes, back in the days when they
lay like fallen leaves in unseasonal descent
          on city streets

a visiting friend from early years was appalled
       by the callous way in which
          I stepped over

       fellowmen abandoned to
alcohol or drugs or diabetic coma
          and decided

his heart had not hardened to the needs of others.
          He would not pass
       another soul in despair.

       The next one lay on his back
          in peaceful sleep.
He shook him awake and asked if he needed help.

The man tried feeble punches and called me by name
          to give him help
       against the guy shaking him.

       I asked him when he had stopped
          taking his meds
and how many pints of vodka a day he drank.

       For the misunderstanding
my friend donated twenty dollars, an amount
          not disputed.

ADVICE TO THE POLICE ACADEMY

I felt I would be attacked
by two loitering malcontents who looked somewhat
tougher than me.

With no escape,
I made no attempt to sidestep what seemed my fate
and looked them cold in the face.

Lawmen's predatory eyes
returned my gaze
and neither made a move as I walked slowly by.

Street attackers nearly always avoid your stare
and look sidelong
at this or that, up or down.

These two plainclothes officers
had yet to learn
role players can't afford to have judgmental eyes.

Women know it very well:
they estimate a man's potential at a glance
and look away.

PEDESTRIAN CROSSING

A car turned the street corner
       fast and hit
       the bag

of library books I held
       to protect
       my gut.

The books thumped against a door.
       Hit and run,
       no way,

the car stopped. The driver stepped
       out to look
       at me.

I guessed that he might be on
       probation
       and so

he could not take the risk some
       minor thing
       like a

highway code infraction might
       put him back
       inside.

I yelled obscenities and
       shook my fist
       at him.

He seemed much relieved to see
       with his own
       two eyes

that the fool he hit could still
       dance and sing
       in rage.

KNOCK ON THIS DOOR

every hour
until someone
tells you something.

Do not do
what this person
tells you to do

because this
may be
psychosis.

NOVEMBER

The wind has stripped the leaves from their tops
        and now the November trees
display any leaves still intact and
        youthfully jump in the wind
        like men prematurely bald

&

        The two poodle-shaped dogs have
        a light golden fur almost
invisible in the golden leaves
as they bury their noses and run,
        creating parallel wakes

SWEET ASSASSIN

Passport photos in rows
on a newspaper page
in color, eleven
men and four women, some
better in appearance
than others, two or three

might even have problems
with personality,
faces average you
could say for almost
any group except for one
face that jumps out at me.

Her eyes are large and brown,
her lips are sensual
and have a humorous
upturned personal twist
that suggests intimate
contact and whispering.

These passport photographs
show foreign visitors
that intelligence claims
are hit team members who
smothered an arms buyer
with his hotel pillow.

I think she needs to hide
and now I have her here
beside me naked on
my bed and doing things
that I will not inflict
on you, my listener.

We rest a moment, skin
to skin, and this is when
she turns confessional
and whispers in my ear:
Darling, there is something
you should know about me.

SORTING MAIL

I noticed a man in a dark suit
climb the entrance steps in front of his
private home on a Manhattan street,
unlock the outer glass-paneled door,
unlock the mailbox, turn around and
come outside with a handful of mail.

He raised the lid of the garbage can
and placed it to one side, examined
each envelope as if its contents
were seeping through and discarded most
unopened as if denying home
entry to highly odorous fish.

Although I don't own a home, I thought
a method like this could work for me —
were it not for the fact that I know
I would have to return to the can
in less than twenty minutes or so
to retrieve needed pieces of mail.

RESPONSE

Your eyes do not work
like a camera.

Your brain constructs its
images with what
you already think.

A quarter of all
brain activity
is involved in this.

You think these poems
are like photographs.

2

LIKE IT IS

He was surprised, a public relations man,
to be asked to speak at the graduation.

He put together what he thought was needed
for graduating Americans to hear.

A colleague remarked, You think God may want them
to die for Wall Street – they will not accept that.

He tried a rewrite but it said the same thing.
On a very early train north to the school

he had no ideas. He sighed and picked up
the New York Times. Six stories on the front page.

He recognized who had placed four of the six.
Here was his speech! These kids don't know what's out there.

Do they think reporters fan like honeybees
from the busy Times hive in search of stories?

And whose thoughts can they expect to influence?

Men who beat pizza dough and know what they know
or readers proud of their independent minds?

UNDERGROUND

Beneath the twigs and bitten grass
the blue and yellow rioters
pushed and hosed are struggling upright
in knowledge that their time is come
and that they cannot now be stopped

the crocuses are shouldering
the winter soil restraining them

SURPRISED BY GULLS

She took crusts of bread to feed the sparrows
on foot-thick snow beside the East River.

The ring-billed gulls wheeled around, clamoring,
wingtips at times almost touching her face.

I saw two young men ahead, without coats
at freezing point, lean on the rail and look

out over the water – to me it seemed
an unlikely pause to admire the view.

They waited for us to pass beyond them
to where the path through snow had no escape.

When I called to her the excited screams
of gulls around her head drowned out my voice.

She threw crusts in the air quite near the men
and the gulls mobbed them with frantic circling,

backing them away. She returned to me,
bread exhausted, and we retraced our steps.

Again they looked out over the water,
again resumed their predatory wait.

THROWING OUT A BOOKCASE

A lightweight ramshackle bookcase
being carried by two women,

all legs and arms, bare and shapely,
out the door of an apartment

on the ground floor blocked my entry
and I volunteered assistance

to discard it on the sidewalk
and joked with them on their reading.

They were busted six weeks later
with whips, handcuffs and rubber stuff

and with the man who often sat
alone in a car parked in front.

I heard he ran the show inside
without setting foot in the place.

And now what about the bookcase?
Look at it from their point of view:

what could they do with a bookcase?
No one is as kinky as that.

LATE AFTERNOON, FIRST AND 88TH

She walked her walk in high-heeled boots with dangling pom-poms,
a grown woman, much beyond the youth, probably high,
who stooped behind her and tried to catch the bobbing playthings
as she strode beyond his reach without a backward glance.

He straightened up and turned for approval to his friends,
five of them, their schoolbags on the ground, who had held back,
all of them near six feet tall and almost two hundred pounds,
none showing a wish to rob, molest or interfere.

If he had knocked the woman to the ground the charge could be
assault and while she and he were white, his friends were black
and although this was Manhattan not Alabama
nonparticipation might not be enough in court.

As I approached, I thought up friendly words to warn them of
the legal risk of such nonprofit activity
and noticed them step backward and look another way,
clearing the stage for a thing about to happen here.

Had he surprised me, my white assailant would have downed me –
I moved with him and tried to bang his skull against a car
and though he broke away I was satisfied to have
communicated in language I think they understood.

APRIL IS HERE

The buds are budding,
the daffodils are popping

and I imagine an earthy smell
in the springtime city air

in which there is a little chill
but one that does not interfere

with women in a backyard laughing
who sound as if they have been sipping

HOSPITAL TOMATOES

Each morning doctors arrived with tomatoes handpicked behind their suburban
                    homes
and looked for city-dwelling colleagues to appreciate taste ripened on the vine.

I carried four bags home and had to look for other city dwellers to eat them.

As days passed and we tired of the joys of all at one time ripening tomatoes
if we could we avoided medical doctors approaching us with bags in hand.

A doctor insisted I accept a bag of what he called "rescued" tomatoes
telling me how an hour ago while he stood on his hometown train station
                    platform
he lifted the lid of a garbage receptacle in order to dump his wife's
slowly picked garden gifts only to see it already half filled with tomatoes
and had not the heart to abandon his own bagful of what he called family
survivors that he now trustingly was handing over to my personal care.

TRY LOURDES

A godless psychiatrist often encouraged
patients to visit Lourdes. A miraculous cure
        is what you pray for.

He believed many physical maladies are
secondary symptoms of an underlying
        depressive disorder.

If you can alleviate your depression
your physical symptoms can as if by miracle
        suddenly disappear.

In Lourdes you see the desperate exaltation
of the spiritually aroused, beyond hope
        of a physical cure

through conventional medicine, and their aura
has an oxyacetylene glare that destroys
        the fabric of despair.

You are moving across the stones upon your knees.

NEIGHBOR

            You've seen a brain-damaged man
take occupancy of a place on a street
        where no one demands his removal

            He has his own possessions
which he arranges around himself
and things kind-hearted people give him to eat

You hardly notice him anymore
            seeing him there every day
always in the same place and at the same time

            Until one day you notice
now the sidewalk is clean and empty
and you never see or hear of him again

UNTITLED

He warned me not to step
on any roaches and
to brush them off the chair
before I sat. This was
meant for their sake, not mine.

He never mentioned mice
running all over me,
looking for things to eat
but in a friendly way.

My food stayed unopened:
sliced Virginia ham,
sliced American cheese
and a loaf of sliced bread.

A visit days later:
ham and cheese on the floor,
mice and roaches at work,
mold consuming the bread,

the mice ignoring me
the way golf course rabbits
ignore people with clubs
savagely swiping at
the balls in the grass that
they consume placidly.

THIEVES

Still chained, a bicycle frame
picked clean as a chicken bone.

Thieves contribute to our lives
by keeping them lean and mean.

When they broke into my place,
rooted around and then left

without taking anything,
why did I feel insulted?

DAYBREAK

Before she left I sat up in bed
and promised her I would do that day
a number of things she needed done.

I do not remember this event.

When I said yes to her verbal list
she should have known immediately
that one of us had to be dreaming.

BEFORE DAWN

Before dawn I swig antacid
and look out a window
at people running.

Those raised in the years
of governmental plenty
with benefits galore

to usher them comfortably
out of this world
behave like there's no tomorrow.

Now that hope of benefits
is going or gone
why run in predawn street light

punishing body to extend
life into almost
certain deprivation?

EAST RIVER VIEWS

1
The East River, its turgid
oiled discolored tidal bulk
running against whatnot, deep,
lit by dawn and blown by wind,
ruffles and calms and reflects
thoughts rippling across its brain,
perhaps

2
A pale hand of fog
lifts off the water
and runs its fingers
between the buildings,
careful not to break
those tall and fragile

3
An October afternoon,
among debris outgoing
with the tide, down the river,
beneath the glass-skinned buildings,
a brown goose, head under wing

4
A cheddar moon
in the raspberry haze
low over Brooklyn
other side of the river

5
The plates of ice on the black water
palpitate in the wake of barges.
They slide with the tide and crowd in herds
along the bank, nudge against the dock
and collide – with a high-pitched tinkling.

6
Riverside lights
on black water
make yellow bars
smeared by movement

7
      A pod of kayaks
invades the navigation path of
      a barge pushed upstream
           almost submerged with
its load of liquid hydrocarbons
      and another barge
           being towed downstream
its bulk completely out of water
      weightless emptiness

8
The green light to port
and red to starboard,
the barge is coming
directly at you

3

VOLUNTEER

I offered to wash the dishes. I claimed
I had professional experience
in this field, although none recently,
      I was happy to say.

Some implements that I took in hand
bewildered me, and I turned them around
like a future archeologist
      pondering their use.

Do archeologists of the present day,
in the dustfree quietness of long rooms,
ask the people who mop the floors
      or chop vegetables

if they recognize any ancient tools?
Might it have been used to polish oak?
      Or core apples?

NEW YEAR AWAKENING

It was snowing as I waited in line
outside Trader Joe's liquor store
and joked with a woman behind me:
You know you have a drinking problem
when you stand in line in weather like this.

What I said touched a nerve. She left without
a word – I never got to say I was
only joking. I think of her
as dry and happy, as someone who can
weary friends by recollecting
the incident that changed her life.

RADIO TIMER ACCIDENTALLY SET

It was music of a serious kind
and I wondered about the band outside
at nearly six thirty in the morning –
I could see a clock where I lay in bed –
I could hear the music was not moving,
it did not seem to be a marching band
and sounded anyway more symphonic,
not coming from the street as I had thought,
the fifty instrumentalists or so
must be crammed into many tiny yards
behind the houses and I drifted off
considering the logistics of this

IN PASSING

1
Tracey Emin,
the painter, says
that she judged love
by what she got
but now she thinks
she should have judged
by what she gave

2
The Goncourts noticed that nothing is repeated:
not the physical pleasure a woman gave you
one particular time, not an exquisite dish
you ate. You'll never have exactly that again.

3
        As John Berryman
leaped to his death from the upper deck
of the Washington Avenue Bridge
over the Mississippi River
        the lone onlooker
saw that John Berryman waved at him

OUT OF TOUCH

Starved Bolshevik rebels
invaded the palace
of a Russian princess.

They said they'd spare her life
if she showed them the way
to the palace kitchen.

She said she had never
been there and so had no
idea where it was.

George H.W. Bush,
seeking reelection,
tried a supermarket.

The barcoded checkout
amazed him, which told some
he had not bought his food

or household things for years.
The princess was intrigued
by cooks preparing food.

The Bolsheviks eating
were amused: she ended
safely in Switzerland.

The media people
did not smile: Mr. Bush
had to leave the White House.

STRANGE PEOPLE IN SUBWAYS

If you get a seat in a crowded subway car
      close your eyes.
You soon hear a dominant voice, often someone
      standing near
you, a man or woman you cannot see because
      of closed eyes.
Do not open them. Instead, listen to that voice
and visualize the person it belongs to.
      Sometimes I
alarm people when I stare at them amazed at
how they differ from the people I listened to.

AARP: 99 GREAT WAYS TO SAVE!

Plastic shower caps make wonderful food
storage covers, and baby socks, stretchy
and colorful, make cheap cell phone covers.

The American Association
of Retired Persons made these suggestions.
I hear a near family member say:

The first we knew something might be wrong was
when she put plastic shower caps on food
and a little sock on her telephone.

STAR PERFORMER

I worry about
a fearsome nun
in Paradise
sidling up to me
like an Olympic
woman boxer
and saying to me:

I hope it was worth
all those coins you
inserted to light
my corpse in the box
where they put me
in the dry crypt
of that cathedral.

HEADLINE

Eighty six year old woman
falls off cliff while raking leaves.

Ponder a headline like that,
who needs to read the story?

Folk want a happy ending:
caught in a tree branch halfway
down, she was rescued unharmed.

And the leaves? They whirled into
a little heap of compost
on which wild strawberries grew.

SUSPICION

She was seeing someone,
he said, he did not know
who but knew when because
she always washed her hair.

Jealously paranoid
was what she would call him
if he confronted her,
a diagnosis that

might possibly hold up
unless he spied on her
and caught her in the act,
a thing he would not do.

SHOPPING CART TRAVELER

We go to countries with language and culture we only
incompletely understand and feel pleasurably
disoriented and sometimes rejuvenated.

At home I wander supermarket aisles and puzzle at
the way the products are arranged on shelves and feel a mind
at work that differs incomprehensibly from my own

as in Tajikstan or indeed in upland Borneo.

TAKING OFF FROM JFK

Just as Zeus
gazed a world away with shining eyes
and allowed

Hector and Trojans to rage outside
Troy's ramparts
near the blackened hollow hulls of Greeks

you tighten your seat belt and peer down
as earth sinks
under your immortal feet at how

Manhattan's cardiac engine pumps
its pulsing vascular arteries
beneath you

and you see the logic of places
in relation to one another
like a god

like Zeus you
let Achilles sulk in a highrise
and turn your shining eyes to a coast

where starlets
who live on ocean breeze and yogurt
romp in surf

AUDEN ON LOWER EAST SIDE

The face of W.H. Auden
was unmistakable even when
it was attached to a coatless man
who jumped as only alpine goats can
from hardened snow to garbage frozen.

A loose-knit scarf perhaps fifteen feet
was wound around his neck as he jumped
about St. Mark's neglected sidewalk.
I said, Good morning, Mr. Auden.

Yes, indeed, he said, wondering who
I was, and leaped in carpet slippers.

ON FIRST HEARING FRANK O'HARA

Late for the reading: I stopped for a drink with friends, one drink
led to another. The dais and lectern are empty.
The auditorium is full and I have to wonder
where Frank O'Hara might be. There he is, empty-handed,
standing in the front row. People pass him sheets of paper
and he reads from them. These definitely sound his poems,
not theirs, although he reads with a humorous detachment
as if they might have been. He has what's called a preppy look.
I've never been to a reading with an empty lectern.

WHAT TO SEE IN NYC

Some people impress visitors
with fine dining in tall buildings.
I suggest the dog-sitting place
on First in the early eighties.

From the sidewalk you have a view
through clear floor-to-ceiling windows
of large dogs in one area
separated from smaller dogs.

The time to come is after five
when the dogs have tired of playing
and now all stand pointing one way,
looking for owners to arrive.

Owners come singly down the ramp
into canine scan through the glass.
Each dog abandons dignity
upon owner recognition

like someone who has put money
on an outsider at the track
and is now the only person
jumping and yelling in the stand.

REDHOOK

A young woman opened an all-girls' bar
and saw no reason to pay protection
        in Redhook, which is Brooklyn.

The watchful men who don't make any noise
        might have knocked around a guy,
with this woman they always took her car

every time she parked and always left it
legally parked not very far away
        in Redhook, which is Brooklyn.

BEETLE

A white beetle climbs one side
of the slender black building
taller than its neighbor,
the United Nations.

Visible far away,
the beetle must be huge.
It may have suction cups
on the tips of its legs.

You think it's a window washing
cable-suspended gondola.
I look again. It's a beetle,
maybe the largest of its kind.

LOOKING OUT THE WINDOW

1
How wild our animal life can be
can not be a thing we think about.

What could have happened did not somehow
and we are alive to tell the tale

or not but not unhurt. Them and us.

2
This place is only that, a place,
no matter what it reminds us

of, and nothing more, only that,
a place, in which we are alone,

a place to walk in single file.

3
Irrational exuberance can be
words we immediately understand,

and what they mean to you they mean to me,
a thing we do not need to think about:

a complex gladness at feeling alive.

4

AT TIMES SQUARE ON NEW YEAR'S EVE

A hundred thousand faces
look up at the open stage.

Four degrees below freezing,
she flashes her bare midriff

beneath a white fur coat and
red spangled top and leggings.

She sings and young women in
the crowd mouth her words and smile –

this is the way they feel too
if anyone would listen.

MUST SIGN

To have four poems published in a
state-funded literary journal
I must sign that I have no current
financial transactions with Iran
and that at least five years have elapsed
since I was released from doing time
on any felony conviction.

Admit it, poets are dangerous.

People thought bankers harmless and dull –
now they think they should all be in jail.

What if an ayatollah sends me
a bag of money for a poem?

A CAUTIONARY TALE

A writer prided himself
on being able to turn his hand
            to anything.

His literary agent
got him one title in a series,
            a trial run

because the editor was
unsure an author of men's fiction
            could deliver

a smart woman detective
for a genre female readership
            convincingly.

He found scalloped collars, fake
furs and shoes described in ad copy
            in magazines

and sent the detective to
embassy parties, restaurants and homes
            for dogs and cats,

added feminine touches,
liked what he had done and submitted
            the manuscript.

No woman would ever wear
such clothes, the editor said, at such
            a time of day

or such a place, no woman
that she had ever known would react
            in such a way.

She finished by claiming she
was amazed at how little he knew
            about women.

FOR TWO VOICES

SHE
A hundred miles to drive.
Want to hear some music?

HE
Girl groups wailing about
the way guys treated them?

SHE
And I don't want to hear
guys ranting about how
they beat up their women.

HE
And so we drive onward
in a peaceful silence.

SHE
Remember those old time
Japanese poets you
liked? When one said something
another continued
the thought, then another.

HE
They drank rice wine. That helped.

SHE
Then drink a beer. I'll drive.

HE
I'm good. Why don't you start?

SHE
Anna brushed her cheek on
a yellow wildflower,
not picking it because
it might be endangered.
Its scent reminded her
of a walk with Liam,
whom she desperately
was trying to forget.

HE
She jerked the wildflower
from her face when she saw
a bee emerge. It seemed
large for a honeybee.
Never before had she
met with a killer bee.

SHE
The bee, buzzing around,
had no wish to sting her.

HE
Or so she thought. The thing
performed a killer bee
war dance to summon all
its hive mates for the kill.
The swarm arrived and they
tried settling in her hair.

SHE
Liam had been searching
for her. He ran to help.

HE
Until he saw the swarm
and ran the other way.
The bees took after him.

SHE
She telephoned for help.
A tear ran down her cheek.

HE
Go smell a wildflower.

SHE
Still ninety miles to go.

MICKEY ROONEY ON BROADWAY

As buses unloaded women
from suburban theater clubs
for a matinee performance
with Mickey Rooney as the star performer
outside a Broadway theater

a friend who had the chunky build,
modest height and ethnic background
of the great man himself stopped and
performed an improvisational sidewalk
imitation in song and dance

only to be interrupted
by the great man himself, who said
"Nah, kid, you know you got that wrong"
and did a star performance self-parody
that wowed the visiting women

MANHATTAN GEESE

The Con Edison steam-generation plant site
on Manhattan, south of the United Nations,
exposes gravel, outcrops of schist, ponds and weeds
before piles are sunk for luxury condominium construction.

Two Canada geese walk through the weeds, one ten feet behind the other,
necks extended vertically, heads twitching from side to side,
on full alert. Most of these geese are relaxed around humans
and even approach people with supermarket shopping bags.

What is their problem? Their heads progress through the weeds
like submarine periscopes. They pause before they cross an open space.
Five tennis-ball-size goslings enveloped in down
dart here and there for tidbits and then fall in line.

HEN

For five years she had been paying
eight dollars a month to sustain
a hen in Nicaragua
and now the bird looked different.

In before and after photos
a white hen was pecking the ground,
nondescript for Nicaragua,
no orchids and no bananas.

They looked two different birds, one
a replacement for the other,
the life expectancy of hens
being low in Nicaragua.

Before these words escaped my mouth
I saw the look her girl friend gave me
and my silence acknowledged her
emotional intelligence.

AT THE METROPOLITAN MUSEUM OF ART

1
A painter tells me he will very soon be forced
        to throw out his unsold canvases
        accumulated over the years
        because they occupy working space.

He foresees a public television program
        about a sanitation worker
        accumulating over the years
        a thrown out canvases collection

that he plans to donate to an art museum
        in a building to be named for him.

2

A girl in the Metropolitan says,
In these museum portraits, I suppose
I hardly notice the foreground figures,
the ones the artists were paid to compose,
and look instead at background trees in rows,
lakes, guitars, archangels, dogs in corners.

He was a king and *she* was an empress?
They look like people on a city bus,
the kind you hope won't sneeze on you or, worse,
contrive to rub their bodies against yours.

3

Twelve hundred years ago Yuan Chen
          told his friend the poet
Po Chu-i that he had seen a poem
brushed by him on the outside wall of an inn

and had to use his expensive coat
          to wipe away the moss
hiding some calligraphic characters
in order to read the complete thing.

No one previously bothered to do so,
          Po Chu-i responded,
hypersensitive in that way in which
poets react to well meant comments.

Imagine rival poets back then
          defacing poems, and
every now and then offended authorities
must have ordered walls to be painted clean.

Does moss gather on street art today?

4

Should I tell the Metropolitan?

A woman stares inside a glass case
at a foot-high seated Buddha, brass,
body substantial but not obese,
unsmiling, Indian not Chinese.

 My God, she says, the eyes are exact –
it is definitely Gertrude Stein.

BACKYARD PARTIES

On weekend summer evenings
beyond maple leaves outside
my windows you hear parties
getting under way behind
other apartment buildings
in yards the size of big rooms

Early you hear male voices
assert themselves but later
after they have had some drinks
female voices and laughter
are the sounds that resonate

At one party this summer
people were so quiet we
wondered if they might belong
to some religion that frowns
on wanton display of joy

No bottles and no glasses
but then in the silent dark
we saw passed from hand to hand
something that glowed a moment

ELEGY IN McDONALD'S

Eight hundred million people are hungry
and a billion people are overweight.
Cheeseburgers, fries and sodas or milkshakes

we can afford to buy and this is what
keeps us going from hour to hour, from year
to year, forfeiting our earning power

to nettle and seaweed eating people
(the rich get thinner and the poor fatter)
and being cognizant all the while that

our people are condemned to extinction
with arboreal alarmed-eyed lemurs
and lugubrious weeping elephants.

ROYAL VISIT

William went to spend the day
with President Obama
while Kate visited a school
for little girls in Harlem.

All the girls had been to see
the Disney movie *Frozen*
and they had made in advance
a gift for Kate's baby son
in London, but now drew back,
all seemingly unimpressed.

It dawned then on a teacher:
Kate did not have a long dress,
yellow hair or tiara –
the children could not believe
she was a real princess.

When it was explained to her
Kate amused tried to convince
a critical audience.

5

SHIRT POCKET

There is beach sand in the breast pocket of his white shirt.
He can't remember when he wore it last. What was he
doing on a sand-covered beach in a fish-white shirt?

Was it the time he walked with that beautiful woman
down by the water after dinner beneath the palms?
How long ago was that? He didn't own this shirt then.

It is definitely beach sand. Unless some person
has troubled to produce a convincing replica.
It is possible he is losing his memory.

He intends to look in his pockets from time to time
for items that indicate he indeed has been in
places that do not immediately come to mind.

TWEED

In days when men who worked in publishing houses
wore tweed suits, I wore a heathery tweed that would
not die. I threw away the pants when the legs frayed.
Years later I wore the tweed jacket and blue jeans
into I forget the name on Sixth Avenue.

A man with eyeglasses pushed high on his forehead
and a tape measure draped around his shirt collar
gazed at the jacket, tested a lapel and said,
This you purchased from us.

He said he remembered buying the bolt of cloth
on a rocky isle off the west coast of Scotland
after crossing rough seas in a tiny ferry.

Stonechats, wheatears, red-beaked choughs playing in the air
and calling to one another, gannets diving
and great gray seals watching with their brown doglike eyes.
(Details supplied by me.}

After talk with a weaver in a stone cottage
and more negotiations over smoky malts
in the harbor pub, all parties reached agreement
the bolt of cloth would make its way to the New World.

On his trip back to the mainland, the waves were high
and he nearly broke his arm against a bulkhead.
The heathery tweed showed up at Sixth Avenue.

He hadn't thought about this cloth in a long time.
Now, if I didn't mind, he needed to sit down.

NOTHING TO DECLARE

Green for Nothing to Declare:
a customs agent beckoned
and had me open my bag.

He found nothing and nodded.

In my twenties, I told him,
I frequently used to be
examined but this had not
happened me in quite a while,
what made him stop me today?

Federal regulations
did not permit him to tell,
but he could guess, sad to say,
whatever made them stop me
in my twenties was not what
made him delay me today.

FIFTEENTH DAY OF CHRISTMAS

Outside a tall building
in mid January
a tree stands in flower.

Its roots soaked in hormones?
A steam pipe underneath?
Is it global warming?

The wintry sun catches
plastic unlit blossoms
of wired decorations.

SPRING

1
In frigid cloud-enshrouded March
in apprehensive tone of voice
a radio announcer claimed
only minutes ago he'd seen
on his way to the studio
a big yellow thing in the sky

2
It's getting near mid April
and I think I must agree

that with no blooms or leaves
and hardly any buds

the trees, with idle branches,
look as if they have connived

to take a year off work

3
Enjoying a warm April afternoon
a skin and bone body on a park bench
strokes his or her miniature dog's head
protruding from adjoining nylon bag

4
His bicycle leaned against the wire mesh fence,
which he had somehow managed to climb over.

About eighty, white hair neatly cut, a tie,
he sat at the base of a flowering tree,

pink cherry, with many daffodils around.

The song he sang might have been a madrigal
or something formal in another language,

although you would have to say his voice was weak.

COUNTRY MUSIC RADIO ON MOTHER'S DAY

Listening to country music radio
on Mother's Day is a radical thing to
do. One mother would never close her eyes till
all of her teenage kids came home, regardless
of the hour. Years on, when it was time to go
she lingered on and she said she could not leave
until all of her kids came home one last time.

The last one there, to make a guess, was the guy
doing the song, who sounds like he might have been
on a tour of Alabama roadhouses.

So, now that her sons and daughters had gathered
around her bed in her home, what did she do?
She died with our Savior's name upon her lips.

BREAKING NEWS

Enormous numbers of golden brown butterflies
fly north out of Mexico over the border.
For what purpose? Why are they coming? To breed. True!
Swarms arrive in our country with one thing in mind –
to have sex and lay eggs and leave caterpillars.

RECENT ADVANCES

I hear researchers can now assign
particular neurotransmitters
to specific lines of poetry
and ID the hormones borne in blood
responsible for verbal constructs.

Think what this does for diagnosis.

Seeing a poem, an editor
will now have time to warn the poet
of a medical emergency.

A COUPLE

From up here I see their backs and both may be
gone twenty but little more. He flops around
almost like a child while she takes little steps
and is in control of their trajectory.

In years to come she will call attention to
speed limit signs or approaching traffic lights
and he will wave a hand or just shake his head
about to say please leave the driving to me.

STREET SENSITIVITY

1
When two of them collided
each ignored the other and
went his way without a word:
it was nothing personal.

I would have put my money
upon an instant showdown:
curses, insults, quick punches,
kicks while down, nothing fatal.

These guys avoided conflict:
there would always be a time
good to pick a fight worth while —
and not a loony attack.

2
Did I see aggression
where none was intended?

A lack of good manners
unnoticed by one with
a lack of good manners
I saw as aggression.

He lay on the sidewalk,
his look was bewildered,
he had no idea
what made me put him there.

It had been a random
attack, someone deranged.

DRAMA

A thin agile man in his late twenties
confronted four men in their late thirties,
all beefy guys used to physical work,
one of them superintendent of a house
across the street.

They may have objected to his chaining
his bike to the rail outside the building.

The superintendent advanced upon him
and the thin agile man jumped in the air
and with the toe of his right shoe firmly
tapped the big superintendent in the chest
and landed in good balance on his feet
as the heavyset man hit the asphalt
on his back like a feather dropped by wind.

The big man sat up and watched the thin man
unlock his bicycle and ride away.

The other three could easily have rushed
him and presumably overcome him.

They did not move.

I think we all felt a small tap in the
solar plexus.

DOORBELL

My doorbell is pressed downstairs
at an early morning hour,
someone who can't find his keys
pushing his hand on most of the bells,

someone who sees himself as
a lovable fun person
who shares an environment
with unlovable nonfun persons.

I remember when I was
a lovable fun person
who had friends to remind him
of how often he could be
an unlovable nonfun person.

REALITY

On a bench high above
the East River, folded
jacket and pants, white shirt,
watch and wallet on top,
black shoes placed to one side.

No sign of any note.

I look down at water,
coiling and fast moving.

A man behind a tree
adjusts his camera.

His smirk appears to ask:
what would you have done if
you had not noticed me?

ERRANT SON

The Lexington Avenue local
opened its sliding doors as I passed
the turnstile and rushed to catch the train.

While his mother used her turnstile card,
a boy about three years old escaped
underneath and ran toward the train.

He stood inside the automatic
open doors and smiled expectantly
back at his screaming, running mother.

She and I crossed the platform and got
inside just before the doors slid shut
and the train roared forward on its tracks.

About four stops later, I noticed
that she was still clinging to the child
on her lap and weeping soundlessly

while he tried to extricate himself
from imprisoning arms, impatient
yet pleased in his mother's loving grip.

SUDDEN RECALL

No matter how long
and descriptive or
on the other hand
coded and oblique

what diary can
match an unwritten
found unexpected
motel ballpoint pen?

COAL

1

In Liverpool just after the Beatles
the nineteenth century imitation
Greek and Roman temples that had endured
beyond the Empire were startlingly black.
A fingertip made lines on a white shirt.
There was soot in the air. The sheep were black.

2

In greater Atlanta suppose
every gasoline and diesel
vehicle becomes electric
tomorrow and raises levels
of carbon dioxide in air
because of the increased demand
on power stations fired by coal.

3

Are we on a path to become a multiplanet species
or not? asks Elon Musk. If we're not … we'll simply be hanging out
on Earth until some eventual calamity claims us.

The first humans to emigrate to Mars
are our best hope for the survival
of our species, says Stephen L. Petranek.

Sooner or later we must expand beyond this
blue and green ball, or go extinct, says Chris Impey.

If it's too expensive to process effluent coal smoke
will an exodus to Mars be a cheaper way to go?

CATS IN THE WAY

Cats lie in doorways oblivious.
They don't believe they are camouflaged,
they don't play dead and they are rarely
belligerent things unaccustomed
to give way. Dogs, rabbits and mice see
and understand. But not cats. They all
stay where they are, even the smart ones.

Cats have been watching since Egyptians
built the pyramids. The problem is
what we do makes little sense to them.
If you point at something for a cat
it looks at the tip of your finger.

BY EAR

A knowledgeable person might have named
the Italianate rustic style in which
the house was built and might have known why it
was close to railway tracks. The local stop
was gone – this had been the station house – but
not the trains, they sped by and shook the house.
She said her husband and she no longer
noticed them, although once he had woken
and asked what had happened to the five-ten,
it had not passed through. That day no trains came.

We come in low over suburban roofs
at an early morning hour, do they wake?
Too many flights for them to miss one plane.
Do they ever wander their silent homes
saying yes they've heard the airport is closed?

INSTRUCTIONS

Please take this shamrock to President Obama.
It will surprise him since it's not St. Patrick's Day
or he may assume it must be once he sets eye
on shamrock if he recognizes it as such.
If you decide to fly to Washington DC
you can fool sniffer dogs by putting the shamrock
in a ziplock plastic bag. Please try not to be
ostentatious, but you and I differ on this.
At the White House, don't jump the fence and sneak inside.
They might shoot you. Join a group and leave the shamrock
somewhere Barack will find it. I'll write him later.

BACALL

Lauren Bacall, long after her book
appeared, from time to time, unannounced
came by her publisher's ladies' room.

An editorial employee
very young but beautiful and tough
much in the way of Lauren Bacall
told me she lingered there to observe
what the great star would put on her face.

Bacall snarled, Get the hell out of here.

How had Bacall-to-be responded?

She said, I got the hell out of there.

BBC WORLD NEWS

The BBC reporter in Athens
covering the Greek financial crisis
when first we saw him was white and timid
and behaved as if he felt out of place.

As the weeks passed with Greek politicians
in irate endless negotiations
the BBC reporter in Athens
unbuttoned his shirt and worked on his tan.

The blue sky, the sun, his deepening tan
and the Parthenon over one shoulder
made it hard for TV viewers to grasp
the worsening hardship of Greek people.

POOR MEN FISHING

Poor men on a river bank or ocean pier
catch and keep tiny fish to consume alone
in a smelly room, and some have memories.

When in the mood to talk one might say to you,
You never know what a place is truly like
until you have to make some money in it.

You say you understand but circumstances –
he is not listening, he has fish to catch.

THIS PAINTING

I do not like this painting. Move on,
you say, and look at something else.
Since it is hung here in this museum
the painting may be better than you think.
If it's OK, it's you who are at fault.

Before I move and look elsewhere
I concede this painter I do not like
has imagination. Everyday
imagination surprises us
with an insight or description.

He has that and also talent
in handling brush and colored paints
plus a knowledge of what has gone before.

Imagination ... talent ... knowledge ...
I do not like this painting. Move on,
you say, and look at something else.

IN THE WORDS OF JOEL OPPENHEIMER

People think I am someone
who can be friendly one day
and can ignore you the next,
the kind that runs hot and cold.

Look how thick these lenses are.

Thing is, I don't see your face –
but say Hi Joel to me,
I will know you by your voice.

FANTASY

You don't own me.

               I never thought I did.

You've certainly behaved as if you did.

That was only fantasy.

             You believe
in fantasy?

       Only to do with you.

It's in your mind, nothing to do with me.

I fantasize that you want only me.

Because I am attractive to others
and they come after me.

              Indeed they do.

You know what people say about water –
drink your fill but don't drown.

              I think I drowned.

You think?

       Where will I find a woman as
beautiful as you?

        That's all in your mind –
treat any woman as beautiful and
she will fulfill your wildest fantasy.

And if I do not think her beautiful?

That is caused by your lack of fantasy.

FREE CAKE

I visited her apartment
after work in a suit and tie,
and the doorman once he knew me
merely gestured to the elevator.
But one day he did not let me enter
when I wore faded jeans and a T-shirt.
I said that I had seen people
enter wearing similar clothes.
He knew my voice. By sight, he had
not recognized me. He apologized.

A block north of Lincoln Center
(the Metropolitan Opera House)
there used to be a record store
on Broadway. Outside it one afternoon
a bearded man in a Hawaiian shirt
cut a slice from a huge sponge cake,
ceremoniously placed it
on a paper plate with a plastic fork
and offered it to passersby,
saying that this was his birthday.

Although he stood at a table
on the sidewalk a block north of
the Metropolitan Opera House,
people would not have expected
to see Luciano Pavarotti
clad in a blue Hawaiian shirt
putting a slice of yellow cake
on a paper plate with a plastic fork,
even if they knew it was his birthday.
Not one of them recognized him.

Before Midnight

1

WHO YOU NEED TO START A RIOT
(*after Mark Granovetter*)

One, someone who will throw a rock
if provoked before a window.

Two, someone who will throw a rock
if somebody else throws one first.

Three, someone who will throw a rock
if the others throw their rocks first.

Four, someone who will loot the store
if the others break the window.

FELLOW PASSENGER

A man in a suit, about thirty,
sitting next to me in a slow bus,
loudly and incessantly expounds
on takeovers, buyouts, rate changes
and so forth, sufficient to make me
wonder whether there is anyone
on the other end of the phone call.
There seems to be someone. But why is
this loudmouth in an expensive suit
sitting in a slow truculent bus
next to someone like me? He expounds
on hedges, economic slowdowns,
index funds, low risk blue ribbons. Fuck!
He quickly glances, then continues.
Loudly and clearly I repeat: Fuck!
I have to go, the man tells his phone,
you may have heard, I have a problem.
He gives me a sidelong look and asks,
Are you satisfied now? I say, Yes!

GIVEN A LIFT

As he drove the car
it was annoying
and then alarming
how she said to him
at the traffic lights:
It's red. It's turned green.

In a while she said,
It takes both of us
together to drive.

As he drove the car
were things black and white
like an old movie?

Or yellow and blue
like under water?

MY OPPOSITE

On a floor of a neighboring highrise,
a dog (a terrier, I think) has been
yapping nonstop from eight in the morning,
when its owners abandon it for work,
till six in the evening, when they return.

If it came from an animal shelter,
until now it has never been alone.

Ten hours' nonstop barking, three days of this,
I would have said it is not possible.

A filibustering politician
can allow himself a glass of water.
Not this dog. No granules of food either.

And then on the fourth day there is silence.

Have they had its vocal chords cut or has
it ended in the river? It may have
been returned to a local Puppy Land.

I tell a friend about this and she says,
You should know that dog is your opposite:
when you're left alone you quieten down,
you do your barking with people around.

KEVORKIAN

She would have been more comfortable
with Ralph Lauren or with Calvin Klein
than with Dr. Jack Kevorkian.

How was she going to get through lunch
with a man who said he enabled
sick people to terminate their lives?

She took him to a French restaurant, which
he refused to enter, pointing to
a yellow M down the avenue.

This place is amazing, she enthused,
I've never been in a McDonald's
before, I just can't believe I'm here!

Was it an act or was she sincere?
After all she was a journalist.
He was where he demanded to be.

GALLERY OPENING

I do not remember the name of the gallery
below ground level on I think it was Mercer Street.

After visitors came down a flight of metal steps
they saw wine on their left and plates of food on their right.

Glass in hand, you could watch them descend the metal steps
and forecast which way individuals would first turn.

When you were sober you could get a very high score.

A POEM UNREAD

What's your expectation
of a poem unread?

Love? A striking painting
can catch you by surprise.

Not a poem unread.

You have to work to read,
decide to read the thing
with what expectation?

Love? You see the fountain
in your garden or brick
wall outside your window.

What you do not see yet
is a poem unread.

MAXIMUM SECURITY

Four walls, a floor, a ceiling, neon light,
twenty-three hours solitary, one hour
a day outside the cell for exercise.

What would we do with no one to talk to?
Can this be why at times we wake in fright
at all the steel and concrete in our day?

GOING

Ask what keeps us going.
We drive up close, slow down,
it's death keeps us living.

Death a motel that keeps
a light in the window,
where we shower and sleep.

When you are near you smell
her skin and then you feel
her magnetic fingers.

WAR STORY

Gettysburg sounds like it might have been
in World War II, you could look it up.

When the woman said that as a child
in London she had been terrified
by German bombs, people looked at her
as if somehow she had just stepped out
of a Matthew Brady photograph.

In an undertone a man told those
standing near him at the opening
that she had been a child commando.

She had landed by glider behind
German lines in Normandy, a blade
held crosswise in her tiny white teeth.

SS men patted her head and died
like pigs, squealing in their own warm blood.

It was minutes before the story
got back to her. Even then there were
those who nodded at her denials.
What could she be expected to say?

AT THE NATIONAL ENQUIRER

This is Mr. Sinatra,
let me speak to Mr. Pope.

Ah, Mr. Sinatra, you
want to speak to Mr. Pope.

Mr. Pope shaking his head.

Sorry, Mr. Sinatra,
he is not in the office.

He walked into that office
less than five minutes ago.

You know that he walked in here
less than five minutes ago.

Generoso Pope puts out
his hand for the telephone.

I gesture that I should leave
but Mr. Pope shakes his head.

Hi Frank, sure Frank, see you soon,
he hangs up and then he says:

Kill the Sinatra story.

WEEKEND WORKERS

The parrot called to her until she
answered, and then the bird reassured
continued to hunt from desk to desk
running along tops of dividers
in the empty open-plan office
for things to eat or things to play with.

The white cockatoo allowed his crest
to fall open petal by petal
and screamed at me with a sidelong look
but we knew each other and wasted
no time from our personal pursuits.

Her big apartment was L-shaped and
when she was home and he was awake
but could not see her he kept in touch
through his frequent calls, which she answered.

And outside on Broadway I will walk
voiceless and probably heedless of
the brightly plumaged chattering flocks.

METAMORPHOSIS

It came as a shock when the young woman
with straight yellow hair below the shoulder
sitting demure in the bus suddenly
hand-wrestled with demons above her head
who twisted her hair in a ropelike hank
and let it hang down in a ponytail

HEALTH WATCH

A diminishing testosterone
level in the blood can drive a man
crazy who has been sane up to this.
Men should therefore watch for warning signs.

Could the hawks and falcons that I spot
be only violent fantasies
to compensate for sinking levels?

Peregrine, redtail, even merlin
numbers are up I hear with relief
although it's hard on pigeons and rats.

FIRST AVENUE

As I stroll northward up First Avenue
three or four pigeons
walk next to me in the same direction.
It appears as if
I am taking the air with my pet birds.

The gulls above are
circling on an invisible spiral,
taking easy glides
to enjoy the urban experience.

A guy on a bike
plays just beyond the reach of snapping cars.
His life depends on
drivers with good peripheral vision
and quick reflexes.

Three black sports utility vehicles
flashing colored lights
escort another of their kind unlit
with clouded windows.
A United Nations diplomat hides
inside bulletproof.
I hear the number of cars indicates
the person's status.

As I stroll northward up First Avenue
pigeon companions
walk next to me in the same direction.

AIRPORT SURVEILLANCE

1
People at videos monitor you as you enter
an airport terminal, as they do in big casinos.
They do not wait for you to join the security line,
as they do not wait for you to join a gaming table.
From the start they watch your every move, who you talk to, who
you brush against, what you drink, what you read, all of your moves,
before you think they have even thought about watching you.

2
How can they monitor people in the summer rush
at JFK? They might as well watch bees in a hive.
During busy times they depend on information.
A retired agent in a hospital bed told me
the men at the passport desks are the ones who receive
electronic data on incoming passengers
and push a button on you before you clear your bags.
Traffickers buying freedom or looking for revenge
give data, and so do furriers and jewelers
in Europe who seek the ten percent bounty on goods
seized by customs when not declared for import duties
by women who remove the labels or wear the stones.

2

FIREBALL

Looking north from a window over the East River,
I saw a big fireball, its tail almost vertical,
at ten to one on Tuesday morning. It disappeared
behind the highrise buildings near the river around
72nd Street, a white teardrop. I listened
for the crash, heard nothing, waited for the police and
ambulance sirens, heard nothing – another early
morning incident that passed unnoticed but somewhere
a metallic or stony lump lay too hot to touch
that someone would throw in a bin in the afternoon.

But I had seen it and the cat had witnessed it too.
One day I would say to her, Remember that fireball?
And she would say, Wow.

Huge Fireball over Northeastern US, Google said
later that day, and we recognized our private bit
of planetary theater had been invaded.
It fell in Maine and not on 72nd Street.
I was not drunk. The cat was not imagining things.

THE WORLD AT WORK

I used to see him sitting at a desk
in a window across an open space
looking at a computer monitor
and busily tapping on a keyboard,
which he did for eight or nine hours a day.

The most I managed was four or five hours
and I would not have achieved even this
had I not the goad of his industry.

It never occurred to me that he might
only have been playing video games.

On a bus the other day I noticed
I was the only one not looking at
a telephone and fingering a pad.

Who can they be texting, and what about?

As for myself, I have nothing to say
and just about no one to text it to.

WHO GOES THERE?

Caspar Henselmann
gave me a sculpture,
a length of painted
zigzag sheet metal
too long for a cab.

People said hello
to me on the street,
as if it were a
recognizable
cultural symbol.

It's a matter of
personality
which you prefer – to
hold a lightning bolt
or carry a cross.

AT NIGHT

As the bell in the great clock bangs midnight
Yeats alone in a tower awaits a ghost
with two long glasses brimmed with bubbling wine,
one for him to drink, one for a ghost to breathe.

A hundred years later poet Carrie Shipers writes
of telling her son there is no monster under his bed
and if the monster is lonely after the child sleeps
he can find her alone downstairs at the kitchen table.

BETWEEN A AND B

Metal tables with umbrellas,
corrida posters in black frames,
a plywood bar, a ground floor room
in a courtyard on East Third Street,
even then these were out of style
but since I had no furniture
it could work as my apartment.

People hit the door and shouted
from two to six every morning
and often would not leave because
I could not lock them out if they
came all this way to buy a drink
but once they had a look inside
they were always willing to go.

FOUNDING PUBLISHER

An elderly man with a bushy mustache,
striped blazer and clean boater who could have watched
cricket in Kent stood in an elevator
of a highrise building on East 50th.

An editor announced in a soothing tone:
This elevator stops first on the twelfth floor.
He stood in front of the buttons and no one
bothered to argue at nine in the morning.

The old gent got off at Knopf on the twelfth floor.
The editor explained: That was Alfred A.
He still visits and he doesn't tolerate
the elevator stopping on early floors.

NO TITLE

Irish for deceit
uisce fe thalaimh
water underground

gaire Sean doite
scalded John's laughter
denying he hurts

even better is
the word in Finnish
pilkunnussija

for comma fucker
someone too aware
of punctuation

SCREAMS

We were outside a school
when she became alarmed
by loud screams that sounded
like a panicking horde.

Kindergarten playtime,
I said. They've been quiet
for hours and need release.

Still unconvinced, she said,
Hard to imagine these
terrible screams coming
from small happy children.

I told her that one time
near an English village
I woke at dawn to screams,
many and agonized.
I had not seen when I
arrived the night before
the sign for Parrot World.

She said, I'd have freaked if
I heard things scream at dawn.

I agreed, screams can be
much easier to take
later on in the day.

LEGACY

I sat next to two elderly women on a bus. One had
a cat in a fabric carrying case,
which was jumping around, agitated.
I said cats do not make good travelers.
Mine doesn't mind, she said, pushing down on its squirming body.
This caused two of us to exchange a glance.

After the cat owner got off, the remaining woman said
she had a cockatoo. She held her hand
up to show it had bitten her fingers.

I said cockatoos can live to eighty.
Mine is thirty, she went on, and I worry what will happen
after I am gone. My son would take it
but his wife – she's a lawyer – she says no.
There's a nice Filipino family on another floor
and the bird comes from somewhere over there.
I copied their name from their mailbox and
gave it to my daughter-in-law to make a change in my will.
The gift will be a big surprise for them.

NOTICE

It can be reassuring to read
next to a red fire extinguisher
the name of the one responsible
on that floor of the office building
for evacuation of the staff
in the event of an office fire.

I remember surprise on reading
my name next to fire extinguishers
at a publishing house where I worked.

After I mentioned this at a lunch
a current employee phoned to say
my name was still on the notices
although I had not worked there for years.

Now we know where to find you, she said,
in the event of an office fire.

SOCIALISTS AND OTHERS

From time to time during a hard winter
I helped women distribute sandwiches
on the Bowery for Dorothy Day
from a Catholic Worker Movement van
because these were gifts with no questions asked
for working men who were down on their luck.

I looked on myself as a socialist,
not a Catholic, though I could admit
Christians went where socialists feared to go.

A man whose loft was on the Bowery,
Mark Rothko, used to complain about how
the country was run. I once suggested,
Why not give away cash as you see fit
to those in need, since you now have money?

You're not a real socialist, he said,
you're what I might call a philanthropist
(only he said fucking philanthropist),
you're talking about personal power
over people instead of a nation
organized on socialist principles.

Dorothy Day had her opinions too,
often about people who volunteered.
I claimed that a woman I was assigned
to accompany had no need of me –
she had loyal protectors on the street
who would attack or kill anyone she
pointed at, including me. Be careful,
Dorothy answered with less than a smile.

MEMORY

I went to visit her in hospital
and brought along a six pack of pale ale,
a gift that simply made her roll her eyes.

Another guy held in one hand a shoot
of open bird of paradise flower.
She never forgot, and neither have I.

ON WHEELS

Girls you might think hardly old enough to walk
in small helmets and colorful scooter clothes

speed at the level of your rheumatoid knee
followed by trotting anxious calling mothers.

These new women who ride the city sidewalks
will make a novel challenge to their new men.

BAGEL PLACE

The old bagel place with the plastic chandeliers,
a window full of tall unflowering plants and
workers who looked like they had served seven to ten

has been replaced by a stark illumination,
an aquarium box with people who say Hi,
but the bagel and scallion cheese remain the same

ALERT

Men in black dangle on ropes
from army helicopters
high above water level

muscular activity
at which we know we excel

but don't know how to prevent
a fifteen-year-old in Tomsk
from hacking the Pentagon

WORKOUT

She was riding a bicycle fast
and holding at the end of a leash
some kind of miniature puffball
bred to occupy half a cushion.

I felt sorry for the tiny brute,
little legs whirring like machine parts,
till I saw the handlebar basket
lined with soft white towels to conduct
the reigning miteweight champion home.

OLD MAN'S PRIDE

It's hard on a guy in
a bus offered a seat
by a younger woman.
Thanks, I prefer to stand.

Pass me on a staircase
and I'll admire your butt.
Don't ask to take my bag.

But if you see me fall
don't leave me there to die.

PROVENDER

A nineteenth century American
kept an iron pot of stew simmering
over a low fire and served visitors
from a ladle to a bowl. Uncooked meat
and vegetables brought by the guests were
dropped in the stew for future consumption.

A version of simmering pot lives on
today in a friend's refrigerator,
from which I was told to help myself to
any or all the cooked items preserved
in plastic bags or wrapped in foil, with none
identified and none with any date.

Another friend warned against eating things
from the freezer, saying she was certain
she had seen things there two years earlier.

CLOSE CALL

She steps in front of a bus,
which jerks to a halt a foot

from her face and telephone.
She steps back on the sidewalk

with no interruption of
whatever she is saying.

Might be at peace with the Lord,
ready to meet her maker.

Or, as Hemingway would say,
could be grace under pressure.

And then, putting thought aside,
there's just plain orneriness.

PADDLEBOARDER ON EAST RIVER

Someone is in the middle of the East River
on a stand up paddleboard, too far to assign
a gender but I guess male from the reckless course
taken down the middle of this barge-infested
waterway of weaving tidal countercurrents.

I was on a sailboat with an outboard motor
once in a harbor mouth facing down an ocean
going freighter, fast approaching and blasting air
from a horn at us, since it could not stop or veer
to one side to avoid us. At the last moment
our helmsman steered aside, gunned the outboard motor,
pleased with having shaken his fist at the mighty.

I assume that the paddler on the East River
is an idiot of some kind. The watermen
will claim they never saw him, and it is even
possible on open water they talk the truth.

LADIES

You expect old men to be tough and glittery-eyed
but there are few of them and so many are slack-jawed

it's old women who appear all over in daylight
who climb subway steps pulling a loaded shopping cart

who burrow down the aisles of crowded moving buses
who lean on you when you do not offer them your seat

who talk loudly in rarely heard mountain dialects
who carry big animals in cat-carrying bags

whose hair has the vivid color used by teenage girls
whose watchful eyes let me know they see me watching them

IN YEARS TO COME

She tells me she is answering my call
from a toy store where she is looking for
something for a seven-year-old boy whose parents
live in the woods and do not allow him plastic.

I admire people who live outside convenience
but not those who force their notions on their children.

She thinks that in years to come this seven-year-old
may be the one to construct
the first all-plastic home among the conifers.

LISTENING

We are listening to the elevators
on the fifteenth floor which make different sounds
ascending and descending and when one stops
on another floor we can hear its doors
slide open and also hear behind apartment doors
voices and other sounds that we can guess at
but when one of the four elevators stops
on the fifteenth floor and its doors slide open
she runs for her life from alien invaders
but then peeks out our apartment doorway to see
what they look like while I say hello and they eye
me warily standing there in the corridor

NO SIGN OF WILLIE

Where cars park on the south side
of Madison Square Garden
abundant marijuana
smoke oozes from a bus size
recreational vehicle
with calligraphic letters
spelling out Willie Nelson
the unique country singer
with a legendary life
on the road and this of course
is a publicity stunt
and Willie himself is not
within city blocks of here

PHOTO EDIT

Here's the photo for the paperback cover,
it reveals the man in Muhammad Ali
although we must erase that mark on his cheek.

Airbrush a flaw in the world champion's skin?

Had he got it in the ring, it would remain –
a heavyweight boxer, yet the only scar
he has on his face, he got from a woman,
a broken plate in a romantic dispute.

REGULAR SHAMPOO

Murumuru butter,
amia oil extract,
exotic vegetables

and tropical berries
complicated my search
for regular shampoo.

A man ahead. A large
butterfly flexed its wings
on his left shoulder blade.

I wondered if this was
like walking a lobster
on a length of ribbon.

I asked, Is that your pet?

He glared. Is what my pet?

The butterfly perched on
the back of your collar.

His hand brushed it off and
it zigzagged in flight down
Lexington Avenue.

He plainly thought that I
had something to do with
this butterfly attack,

attaching no blame to
the huckleberry rinse
he may have been wearing.

3

IN TRANSIT

On the 34th Street platform of the downtown Q
the wood benches offer refuge to men and women
who have no homes but who are watchful of possessions.

They trundle their stuff in metal supermarket carts.
None of them look prepared to make some kind of journey,
they want to stay a little while more and not move on.

DAIRY AISLE

The man who is staring at the yoghurts
may not be as slow-witted as he seems.

His wife is gone and it is new for him
to be confronted with such an array.

HARD LANDING

The overnight flight touches down at dawn
and the young woman seated next to me

takes out her phone and exclaims, Hi, it's me,
I'm back! Then she listens and her face falls.

She puts the phone away and sobs gently.
She says to me, I thought he would be pleased.

I say, It's ten to six in the morning.
It could be that, she says, mopping her tears.

A WORD TO THE WISE

Norma claims she saw my mother yesterday
in Eataly on Fifth and 23rd Street.

My mother loved traditional Irish food
and next month she will be dead eleven years.

If she returns from the afterworld
and pretends to like Italian food

what does that say for the Church of Rome?

CURBSIDE

A boy about four examines an empty hole,
his grandmother clutching his hand and gazing down
in the tolerant way that women look at men
doing something of little or no importance

FOR HER

I signed my book of poems
for a woman I will meet
at a party in a week.

She joked she might assign it
as a book report to one
of her several children.

BEFORE MIDNIGHT

Before midnight at the Bleecker Street stop
of the Lexington Avenue local

where cops hide to grab turnstile jumpers
officially believed likely to be
wanted for murder in South Carolina

two uniformed cops stand in plain view
at the turnstiles causing some of the kids
to stop moving almost in mid stride

and all the kids to stare incredulously
as a cop opens an emergency gate
and beckons each one to come on in.

You OK? That's all they ask the kids
as they let them through. Get help, they tell
an older man. Most are kids without the fare
to get home to the Bronx and here are cops
helping the young to get home safely.

Next day a friend asked, Were they real cops
or actors doing street theater?

You have to wonder which is more likely,
he said, a theater experiment
or something new in police thinking.

DON'T WALK

He has put on weight and his movements are stiff
and he waits for the traffic light to change
before crossing the street. He sees I notice.

These new cars can accelerate, he says,
and though they only fire on four cylinders
they weigh a fraction of old gas guzzlers
and can be upon you in five seconds.

Technology, I say as the light changes.

WOMAN ON THIRD & 85TH

With a nondescript guy about her age,
which is around twenty, she is assertive
in her stance and challenging in her gaze,
nothing unusual – but out of place, clad
in a long green dress down to her sneakers,
a folded piece of lace clipped to her hair,
symbol of an eighteenth century bonnet
and indicator that its wearer is
an old believer firm in her values.
Do Manhattan Mennonites have attitude?

AD

At first he thinks that
she's advertising
a gentlemen's club.

Relaxed on her back,
naked, she displays
long inviting thighs.

He's amazed to read
the ad's for footwear –
is she wearing shoes?

DANGEROUS PEOPLE

Taxi drivers are dangerous people.

He made a right turn without signaling
and a cop wrote him a traffic ticket.

He made negative remarks to the cop,
who answered him with another ticket,
this one for a criminal court hearing.

At court he waited with substance dealers,
girls and boys and what were known as lowlifes.

The judge ran through all the cases quickly,
handing out the same fine to everyone.

Except for him. He was fined twice as much
as anyone else. He asked the judge why.

Because we know you pay, the judge said, and
taxi drivers are dangerous people.

MRI

Hands at side, on your back
on a sliding table
headfirst into a tube,
panic button in reach,
you know you must not move.

The electronic sounds
begin, warble in twos,
go solo, disappear,
reappear as combos
in minimal rhythms,
unplaceable thumping.

Baby bats are crying
for their mothers who call
back, their gaping mouths full
of trapped squealing insects.

A calm tech assesses
the amount you can take.

GRAPES

The green seedless table grapes taste good
though many are as big as small plums
and possibly result from genes
radioactively altered
rather than selective breeding.

The package reads Product of U.S.A.
and Distributed from Bakersfield,
California, which I suppose
eliminates a greenhouse origin
in Russia, China or Albania.

BEANS

Agronomists tested bean varieties
for shelf life, for yield, for insect resistance,
for disease resistance. From drones they measured
growth through greenness of electrolyte pixels.
Infrared cameras showed water content,
indicating bean heat and drought resistance.
When the agronomists were asked how the beans
tasted they said no one had thought about that.

MARATHON

I saw Ed on television run
that moment off the Queensboro Bridge
in the New York City Marathon.

I hurriedly quartered an orange
on a paper plate and watched for him
on First Avenue at 88th.

He was red and sweating and gasping
but forging ahead as I ran out
to join him with a quartered orange.

He gave me a frightened look – only
later did I understand he had
broken the physical barriers

runners must break and in me he saw
a new mental barrier, a friend
with a plate, a hallucination.

But a bite into a cold orange
persuaded him it was as real
as the pain of long-distance running.

WHAT WOMEN IGNORE

Three young women on the sidewalk,
all of the same ethnic background,
walking and talking and laughing,
one with an Islamic headscarf,
the others with free hair, makeup
and clothes that enhance their bodies.

Or two clad in Islamic clothes
and one dressed in a Western style.

Or take any combination,
the result is they talk and laugh.

A man might wonder if the bonds
of women are more powerful
than religion and tradition.

What men impose, women ignore.

If I were to stop and ask them
I do not think they would tell me.

TALK OF LOVE

We look for a spark in talk of love,
something odd, a thing particular,
and those who talk the best can do so
from emotional confusion with
a limited vocabulary

A QUESTION IN PASSING

Five or six small kids are chasing one another
next to the place I have just gotten off a bus
while two fathers stand in discussion unaware
of the possibility their children will run
in front of a bus. Is this a good place, I ask,
for your kids to play? One of them is offended
at a stranger's insinuation of neglect.
I almost say but I don't, It's not what I say,
it's how I say it. My tone of voice. It's only
a matter of rewording the word idiot.

MAPLE

The maple leaves are lemon yellow,
all one shade and all still on the tree,
instead of livid red and orange,
as if they came with no exceptions
to a consensual decision
to stay where they are and go lemon

AT TWO IN THE AFTERNOON

Very tall and very wide, head shaved,
a long black beard, he shouted, pointing.

The small black woman he shouted at
recoiled and warily backed away.

He may have appeared like some demon
out of a white supremacist hell.

He pointed to the purse she had dropped,
which she retrieved with an anxious smile.

He gave me a look like he had done
something he wanted no one to see.

GONE

A friend asked if I remembered when
we came here to drink and talk and dance:
over there was where the bar once stood,
the cigarette machine near the door.

I found this hard to visualize
although I had vivid memories.

In New York you know when you've not been
in a neighborhood for months on end
you find a whole block has been leveled,
one wave of a developer's wand.

Without success I try to recall
the stores and buildings that once stood there.

I admit the probability
that I will vanish without a trace.

CARD

I need a card
for her that says
Happy Birthday

something between
sentimental
and moronic

the only card
appealing says
In Sympathy

HEADS

Probably for some good cause,
attached to the tall railings
of the United Nations
a row of old people's heads
stare out from enlarged photos
four feet high and three across,
weathered and expressionless.

A woman asks who they are.

I say that they were rock stars
back in the nineteen sixties.

She doesn't recognize them.

Her man says I am joking.

She says, But he could be right.

STREET FIND

Security camera film showed two men
by street light approaching a shopping cart
in a midtown Manhattan cross street doorway
and before leaving with the shopping cart
removing a pressure cooker and one
tossing it in the doorway disconnecting
as investigators later concluded
the bomb's clock and triggering mechanism

BAT ATTACK

You say you were attacked by pink bats
on Lexington Avenue,
seven or eight of them flying
in close formation, banking
in flight for U-turns and diving
in sequence on your unprotected
head and shoulders. I believe you.

You understand that your mind
at times plays tricks on you, and you
are willing to accept what
people define as real.
The bats were there, you know they were.
But you accept what this may seem
to others. Because you are sane.

PASSING THROUGH

The anticlockwise storm reaching north
to Labrador has moved out to sea
but its backward swirl now is dropping
a foot of snow on New England down
almost to the city of New York.

Eight or nine American robins
migrating north are doing thrushwork
on muddy grass in Stuyvesant Town,
fuel for their nocturnal travel.

Will they turn back from the wind and snow
or wing it in a hormonal drive?

FROM WATERSIDE

On a footbridge over the East River Drive
from Waterside on Fridays and Saturdays
in the evening like nocturnal animals
young women stream into the Manhattan streets
alluring but knowingly self-protective

and each has individual adornment
appealing to her kind of pollinator

and there are the women I do not notice
whose independence makes them invisible
when they do not draw attention to themselves

WOODCOCK

A woodcock is not a bird you would
expect to hear sing from a treetop.

Bulging eyes on the top of its head,
a long bill to probe the earth for worms,
an orangish belly and short legs
suggest a life lived close to the ground.

Here one lies on its side in tree roots
beside East Eighty-Sixth Street. Last night
it hit a bright light while migrating.

CORTEGE

On a barge on the East River a winch
holds a cable that divers attached to
a helicopter fifty feet below
with five inside, trapped in seat harnesses.

In the dark, the small barge floats downriver
with the current, escorted by six boats,
each with a blue light, like a Venice prince
returning at night to his palazzo.

STILL AROUND

Marilyn Monroe lived at 440 East Fifty-Seventh Street,
a man on the bus says in a loud voice. In his fifties,
he is too young to have remembered her. I saw her from time to time,
an elderly woman across the bus answers him, when I
visited – she mentions a name unfamiliar to me –
who lived across the street from her at number 435.
You saw her in person! He shakes his head in wonder and then tells her,
I know that there were lots of Armenians around here then.
There were, she agrees and goes on to name some of them that she knew.
My father used to swim in the East River in the 1930s,
he says. How could he have known she was Armenian? She must have said
something in Armenian to the woman with her, who seems to have
arthritis. He asks, Is that your sister? It is? This is my brother.
I know it's not unusual for a man with Down syndrome to survive
into his fifties. All four get off the bus at Fifty-Seventh.
Are they longtime residents of rent-controlled apartments in what are now
expensive buildings? Their only link may be both knew that
Marilyn Monroe lived at 440 East Fifty-Seventh Street.

MOTH-EATEN

You might think it was a bullet hole
through one sleeve
and through one side and out the other
of a black cashmere sweater,
a moth caterpillar's pathway,
newly hatched from an egg.

Think of all the baby caterpillars
who waken in folds of rayon,
nylon or polyester
and who starve to death
without sprouting wings.

Or does a female moth
disdain to place her ovipositor
in artificial fibers?

WHO READS MY POEMS?

The only way to flow with the market
is to read – everything, no matter what,
discover what is happening
outside your zone of comfort, take
it all in – not just the people
who buy stocks and bonds
and who make America tick.

After a day on the combine harvester,
having watched Fox News,
he snaps open a can of Bud
and he idly turns the pages
of a magazine
his daughter left on the table.

The wind made running on the beach
difficult today
but now he enjoys the rewards
of extra physical effort,
pours himself a glass of ice cold goat milk and
reaches for a journal crafted
from handmade acid-free paper.

After she examines her skin,
shakes her head to aerate her hair,
sighs over her nails
and tries not to think about body mass,
she reclines and decides to look over
what I have to say about my emotions.

4

CENTRAL PARK RESERVOIR

The cherry tree branches
are in full pink flower
against a spring blue sky.

Eight Asian businessmen
in dark suits motionless
look up at the petals.

Briefcases stand neatly
together on the grass
at a cherry tree trunk.

MINA

Asserting
her hoodedness
of cathood
she lays a paw
down on top
of what she wants
despite her
felinity

DIRECTIONS FOR A DRIVER

I have seen him frequently,
the taxi driver who stops
near the river, takes a mat
from the trunk and kneels to pray.

If I were close I could say:
Praying in this direction,
you are facing Canada.
Mecca is the other way.

SPRING DAY

No more than twenty,
her wool cap pulled down,
a pom-pom on top,
her clothes she could wear
to cross-country ski,
her boots waterproof.

The afternoon sun
is pleasantly warm.

It puts me in mind
of women in line,
a supermarket
in Los Angeles,
some wearing T-shirts
in shorts and flip-flops,
others in fur boots,
insulated coats.

And her taxi will
be air-conditioned.

FORTUNE

He knew or had knowledge of
several big time Wall Street swindlers
and he claimed that none of them
set out with an intention to defraud.

Only after they had gone big time
by going public had they the need
to justify themselves to their investors
in bad times by embroidering the truth.

What later looked like outright lies
they saw they uttered as promises
they believed that they could keep
through confidence in themselves.

When unpredictable events
needed sugar coating for investors
they learned why the Ancient Romans
looked on Fortuna as a fickle god.

A PLACE NAME

The screen of the ringing telephone
reads ATHENS and that could spell trouble –
someone arrested and calling for help
from the city jail. Are Greek jails as bad
as those in Turkey? Maybe someone
who has had her bag and passport snatched?
As I pick up the receiver I read
ATHENS NY. Just someone who needs to know
my social security number
and any account codes I can remember.

GLIDING

Places fall into place when seen from the air,
somewhere you never considered
in relation to somewhere else
you may see almost next to one another
or lying in a direction
you had no reason to follow.

From the uppermost deck of a cruise ship
you have an overlook of waves
unavailable from a drenched
work station on a fishing boat
and of course you can see from a grandstand
what players can't see on the field.

As passenger on a glider
I had not expected the earth
to rush up close to meet me and
then with a gastric shock pull back,
only to rush up close again
and rob me of a godlike view.

BUSY STREETS

It's amazing we don't all kill one another.
You hear this said about city streets known for their
crowds in motion and potential interaction,
often with people who want others to get out of their way
next to people who feel bullied and won't get out of the way.

Some believe authorities should control the streets
and others enjoy the big spectacle and peace –
most feel relieved we don't all kill one another.

MAIN ENTRANCE

A body on the hospital floor.

Someone talked:
Four of them. They were kids. So is he.

Someone talked:
They often leave them outside church doors.

Someone talked:
At least he was not dumped in the street.

Someone talked:
Died of an opioid overdose.

TIMES SQUARE HONEYBEES
(after Kwame Opam in the New York Times)

A cop in a beekeeping veil vacuumed up thousands of loud bees
that were swarming on a hot dog cart on a sidewalk in Times Square.

The Hilton and InterContinental hotels had rooftop hives.

The beekeeper at the InterContinental was adamant
that the Times Square bees were not from his hives. Try the Hilton, he said.

The beekeeper at the Hilton, who also managed the beehives
on the roof atop Ballet Tech, a dance school north of Union Square,
said that to his knowledge none of the Hilton bees had swarmed and that
the hot dog cart bees could have come from the InterContinental.

A Cornell University professor said that there are more
colonies of bees than those in hives. In tall buildings they could be
unnoticed very high up. All they need is a crack in a wall.

Later the hot dog cart honeybees were getting the care they need
in a hive maintained by the police officer who vacuumed them up.

EM AND EN

The capital letter M
exactly wide as it is tall,
a perfect square.

The capital letter N
is half as wide as it is tall,
somewhat slender.

Typesetters back then could see
their logic and honest beauty,
when upside down.

STUDENTS

Until then he had shown little interest
in her opinion about anything,
so now that he was listening fully
to what she had to say about the books
that he gave her, she was flattered – until
she came to realize that these were books
he had been assigned to read and he was
using her to save himself the effort

OVERHEARD

I really don't think that people with long legs
stretch their legs further, a woman with long legs
was telling a woman with much shorter legs
as they slowly walked along a garden path.
There was no way that I could undetected
amble along behind to hear more of what
she had to say about stretching her long legs.

TALL FIN

I may have taken the opportunity
to pee in seawater, not counting on
amino acids in body fluid
attracting a shark, a fifteen-footer
that could lunge at me at more than thirty
miles an hour, while in his open maw sparkled
rows of teeth evolved to tear meat from my bones,
yet who might be stopped if I punched his nose
or drove a fist into his eye or gills,
but knowing I am more likely to be
hit by a car or lightning bolt than a shark
even when urinating in seawater

TEST

A plainclothesman had done all the paperwork
needed to be a detective. He was warned
of other tests he could expect.
                                        A senior
officer outside a courthouse walked with him.
That couple we just passed, what was she wearing?
What was the color of the man's skin, hair, coat?

The plainclothesman got them right.
                                                You were warned.
                                                        Sure,
but I would have noticed those things anyway –
my time as a cop must have messed up my mind.

Knew what was coming and were ready for it –
you seem like the kind of guy we're looking for.

CEMENT

The concrete shell of the basilica fell on
the upturned faces of the joyful hymn singers
in Mexico. Their sound waves shattered the concrete.

This is of course the secular explanation.
Some say it is possible God was punishing
multitudes of sinners in the congregation.

Impossible not to think of concrete crumbling
and collapsing when you look at the building to
the south of Rockefeller University.

It is a massive rectangle perched over the
downtown and uptown lanes of the East Side Highway
on two spindly thin reinforced concrete ridges.

Might there be a chance of divine retribution?
You think God would not mess with the Rockefellers –
too many are up there in His vicinity.

CONTAINERS

At least one barge passes up and another down
the East River every day with a cargo of
dark blue containers painted with scattered white stars,

perhaps conveying dated designer garments
to overlooked undiscriminating markets.

The packaging makes a friend suspicious. He says:

medical waste or radioactive products
to a dumping site in an impoverished state.

DINOSAURS

We like to think a dinosaur could roar.

Imagine a velociraptor chirp
like a frog.

Or did they cluck like hens on their way to
extinction?

And why did these dominant animals
disappear
in such a short geological time?

We think that clouds may have darkened the sky,
blocked sunlight and caused temperatures to
drop, which froze
many cold-blooded reptiles in their tracks.

Even intelligent dinosaurs could
not imagine such a slow chilling end.

And we humans too are finding it hard
to believe
that we might go in a similar way.

No chirping or clucking, we need to roar.

A WINDOW SHADE

Pull down your window shade, a stewardess
says impersonally. Out the window
a jet engine nestles beneath a wing.
Can a plastic shade block the fact that we
are traveling at seven hundred miles
per hour at about forty thousand feet
in the dark above the wild Atlantic?
Such is the comfort of a plastic shade.

A VACANT LOT

A vacant lot on First Avenue
is barricaded with plywood walls,
behind which the trees, tall for their age,
show just how little time they would need
given a chance to reclaim the ground

WOMAN DOWNTOWN

They enjoyed sex together after she
injected what she said was insulin
and had fun together for days before
he learned she was not a diabetic

GLADIOLI

He liked gladioli
and bought many of them
to give her, till she said
during an argument
they made her home look like
a funeral parlor

AWAY FROM TOWN

So you got out of the city
to live in the piney foothills
with breezes from the sea instead
of diesel fumes and cries of birds
instead of ambulance sirens.

It was a shock to hear it would
take fifty thousand bucks to run
electric wires from the highway
only four miles away, and since
the well water always tastes foul
you have to drink bottled water,
coyotes ate your dog and cat,
the wildfire fortunately burnt
up the slope from your place and while
you are still coughing from the smoke
now you have been told a mudslide
just might happen without warning.

Today you saw on your cell phone
(good reception on the other
side of the hill) that crime is down
in New York City, making you
think of lazy hours spent among
gentle people in Union Square.

SECURE IN ITS REMOTENESS

I spell out reminders of
my bank and credit card
digital codes in Irish
and in the monastic script
of the middle ages
for bibles in manuscript.

The script, taught in Irish schools,
is no longer in use,
dreamed up by nationalists
for an Irish-speaking state
with an alphabet that looked
different from English.

My use in New York City
is some kind of epitaph
for script but not language.

POLICE ACADEMY

Inside the Police Academy
voices counting from one to ten, they
begin again.

I say to three cops standing outside,
Listen to that! They're learning to count!

One of them grins but the other two
are not amused.

HOUSEWORK

From the train window we could see
a flat roof with solar panels.
For them to work properly, she asked,
would someone have to clean them often?

CONFLICT

Two warring factions can settle their differences.

Differences are usually not the problem,
Rene Girard claimed,
but similarities between the two warring sides.

In his eyes conflict
is competition and imitative rivalry
between those who are like each other in ways they are
eager to deny.

Settling their differences can be a waste of time.

EMERGENCY ROOM

In the hospital emergency room
with a cut in my right leg,
I am handed a clipboard with four sheets
of printed data, each sheet with a space
marked by a penciled X for me to sign.

I sign the lot without reading any
and return the clipboard to
the observantly waiting attendant.

I say, I think I might have donated
my heart, kidneys and liver.

We are very grateful, he says. And smiles.

Americas

1

FROM WEBSTER'S THIRD
NEW INTERNATIONAL DICTIONARY

hollyhock: a deep purplish red
that is bluer and deeper than Harvard crimson (sense 2)
or American beauty
and redder and duller than magenta (sense 2a).

magenta (sense 2a): a deep purplish red
that is bluer and stronger than American beauty,
bluer, lighter, and stronger than hollyhock,
and bluer and deeper than Harvard crimson (sense 2).

Harvard crimson (sense 2): a deep purplish red
that is redder and paler than hollyhock
or magenta (sense 2a)
and stronger and slightly bluer and lighter than American beauty.

American beauty: a deep purplish red
that is redder and paler than hollyhock,
redder and less strong than magenta (sense 2a),
and less strong and slightly redder and darker than Harvard crimson (sense 2).

PUSH
LLUP

blue sky

t   e   h
h   n   e
i   d   r
s   s   e

another case of that

                grass

the
        semidomesticated
                slow
                        death
                                of
                                        the
                                                stricken
                                                        dove

W ho?
W hat?
W here?
W hen?
W hy?

H ow?

Have you written your account number
on the check enclosed?

Have you signed your check?

Have you enclosed the appropriate
portion of the bill?

Does our address show through the window?

Is there a stamp on the envelope?

Pray for it

Pay for it

ASTRONAUT

Heaven is blue eternity

    around the globe
    above the winds
that drag the clouds in patterns good for weather forecasting
in a cumulonimbus greenhouse atmosphere.

    No vertigo,
    floating

    too high up
to tumble down screaming and waving your arms
in the air-writing reflex of an animal falling.

LEAVES

        Louis grows
    becomes aware
of how the seasons move

        how the leaves
    green on the trees
when the weather grows warm

        fall to ground
    before Christmas
when the weather grows cold

        again are
    back on the trees
when the weather grows warm.

He asks, How do the leaves
get back up on the trees?

THE WITCH AND DAFFODIL

Once ago
in the trees
an old witch
with gray hair
fed pigeons
yellow corn.

The old witch
was covered
with black rags,
the pigeons
thought she was
a tree trunk.

She scooped more
yellow corn
from a brown
paper bag
deep in her
shopping cart.

The pigeons
flapped, circled,
perched upon
her shoulders,
pecked and shoved
at her feet.

The old witch
gazed fondly
on her birds,
little ones,
featherbrains,
gobbling corn.

Along came
Daffodil,
her daddy
taking her
out walking
in the park.

Daffodil's
combed and brushed
curly hair
wasn't gray
and her clothes
weren't rags.

The old witch
saw her and
bared her teeth,
what some might
call a smile,
some, a snarl.

The small girl
danced on the
yellow corn,
the pigeons
panicked, flew
in the air.

Daffodil
laughed, the witch
moaned spells on
one who'd made
her pigeons
fly away.

FIVE MINIATURES

1
snow hare
where?
there!
nowhere
no hare

2
Do the leaves
hang sullen
on the trees?

3
A valentine:

onto a heart
attach six legs
and a pair of
long antennae

4
Out in the black
ether of space
the stars lie hit
like tennis balls

5
You hover at the flower
and drink nectar on the wing
no one knows your devil's name
evil wicked mean and fast

2

PHANTOM INFANT

Weeks before the birth
of her first baby,
she looked down and saw
a phantom infant
gazing up at her
with his father's eyes.

Then he smiled at her,
his sharp little teeth
stood in even rows,
and he said, Feed me.

MARINER LOST

A weekend mariner,
among his friends a font
of navigational lore,
clutches an encrusted plank
beneath a wave the size of Fuji,
in the shimmering depths of which
a finned leviathan
sports an appraising eye.

Through broken cumulonimbus
a shaft of light
bathes the mariner's face.

Mistaking it for
a helicopter's
air-sea rescue beam,
the mariner looks up and sees,
trident upright,
Neptune smile.

NEED

It was when you caught
the rat in the trap
and threw the wire cage
in water
to drown the beast

the rat in the trap
used its head
to force apart the wires
and swam to gasp in air.

It's when you can't open
a painkiller bottle's
childproof top
and you tear apart
its clear plastic skin.

WALK

She walked around the big pond
in the Luxembourg Gardens
feeling she was being followed

quickening her steps and almost
catching a fleeting movement
out of the corner of her eye.

She saw she was being followed —
a golden shoal of foot-long fish
swam in formation behind her

and when she stopped they waited
to be fed milling about
orangely in the green water.

She thought about the friend who lived
in Churchill on Hudson Bay
who had no fear of polar bears

but hated to be followed
with her dogs at the water's edge
by a pod of killer whales.

CRAWL

For fear they hide spiders
no pictures on the wall.

An octagonal home
with no deep dark corners
in which devils can hide.

A scorpion may spend
the night inside a shoe.

A guest wakes in the dark
to feel the brush of fur
upon her skin and shrieks.

The kitten runs in fright.

A SLIGHT EDGE

1
Although there's a sheer
drop of twenty feet
on the wall's far side,
coils of razor wire
assure the tenants

2
His mind so vicious
remarks so cutting

some day he will climb
a water tower

shout down at passersby
while they shoot up at him

3
A taxi brakes to a halt
by the river, the driver
gets out fast and runs away.

Perhaps I should take cover.

He turns around and runs back,
looks upward, stretches, breathes deep,
sits inside and drives away.

4
The bright white ameba core
delicate pink aureole
of an exploding missile
exist a millisecond

a flower that opens up
the innards of a city

MOONS

1
In binoculars
the full moon
orange through
city haze
shows what an omelette
should look like
when perfectly cooked

2
Triton, moon
of Neptune,
small, bright,
cold, pink

SAY IT WITH FLOWERS

Who knows whose idea it was
to sink tulip bulbs at Christmas
at random in the calm acres
of lawn that stretched before the house.

The absent owner was a hailed
authority on Henry James.

According to the photograph
the petals would be all one kind —
jagged bands of yellow, black, red,
a comic art depiction of
hot rod or funny car exhaust.

In spring, in the early morning,
his wife phoned to say that he was
thrashing the blossoms with his cane.

PEN NAME

If you write novels
with action heroes
expect some letters
from mail box numbers
in small towns near large
penitentiaries.

A guy who wrote me
about a combat
book I did was sure
I must have served in
the same unit he
did unless of course

he was bullshitting.

HER WALK

Her walk it goes
like she's unaware.

The traffic grows
as the drivers stare.

Construction slows
as workers compare.

She's wearing clothes.
Imagine her bare.

EARLY MORNING BAUDELAIRE

You know how birds scream their heads off when you
are trying to get a little shuteye
in the morning. I suggest that next time
you find yourself beneath a spreading tree
before the dawn's first light, take the trouble
to blow cigarette smoke into the leaves
above you to irritate avian
bronchioles. And before you leave, be sure
to shake the branches where you think they sleep.

CLOUDS

In these parts you don't often see
big puffy clouds sail one by one
across the blue sky, out of shape
clouds that just haven't looked after
their cumulous bodies – not mist
or wisps elongated along
a globally curved isotherm.

These clouds float like comforting thoughts
and bulge like overstuffed armchairs
against the thin atmospheric
blue of empty space above us.

GOING BACK

        I walked around the town
on streets familiar from other days
but I saw no faces my eyes had longed to see,
no one on the sidewalks, entering stores,
leaving buildings or sitting in a coffee shop.

        I do not say it was
now a horror film alternative town
populated by a variant human form.
I do not even say I did not see
anyone I knew – only none I wanted to.

3

NOCTURNE

Even though there are footmarks on her skin
and the doctors say that she is getting
more unstable, more unpredictable
by the month — she may even be frigid
to her core — there she goes, still hanging out
in her old haunts: I can see her tonight
through the bare branches of a leafless tree.

And in the darkness the frogs make noises
louder than trucks on the distant highway.

SNOWSCAPE

The longboned rock has stuck its knees and elbows through
a tattered coat of snow on the western Catskills.
Across the whitened chamber of a large hollow
the brambles burst like particle trajectories.
A randoming flake negotiates a landing.

Sound bounces down into the valley, hound and dove.
A red plastic bucket leans half sunk in a drift.
Rubber boots stand on a doorstep. At one hill farm
a Ford has buried its nose in a soft hillside,
three cars nuzzle like pups on a great white udder.

NEW ENGLAND GRAVEYARD INVADED BY TREES

Martha Rogers lies alone
underneath a red sandstone,
eighteen ten to sixty-five
were the years she was alive.

On evenings, did she walk this path?
her gingham dress floating over the pebbles,
      silk ribbons flying,
      slender arms, fingers
      throwing back her hair —
who held her breasts beneath the flowering dogwood?
      squeezed a nipple in Maytime?

Silver birch the eye deceives,
nature hides the dead with leaves,
but *her* stone stands, Lord be praised,
others fallen, names erased.

The spirit turns upon the dust:
as imperceptibly as grief the summer lapsed away —
      a great hope fell,
      you heard no noise,
      the ruin was within:
as from the earth the light balloon asks nothing but release,
      she laid her docile crescent down.

The trees and I gather round,
point our faces at the ground,
I ask one, he shakes his head,
all we know is that she's dead.

PEACEABLE KINGDOM

I shake ants from a paper cup
before throwing it on the fire,
which may be out

of respect for natural things,
a nod to whatever powers
reign over campsites in darkness —
may be watching

as ants forage among grass stems.
The chemical-impregnated
paper cup ignites in a flare

that illuminates a woman's
face and arms and hands and ankles.
It may be her

presence that arouses in me
the notion to preserve ant lives
beneath limbs and resinous scales
of the mammoth evergreen trees.

EQUINOX

Fat man in a baseball cap
bottle of beer in his hand
looks up at the starry sky
two a.m. in the darkness
alone in a trailer camp.

Caught in the beam of my light
he gives me an alibi:
think this is the Big Dipper?
know if that is the North Star?

Nobody wants to seem weird
voiceless caught gazing at stars.

OLD PEOPLE WANDERING

Their biological work is done,
they have no more orders for the young,
now they pass like tourists through the place
where they were begotten and begot
in turn, and like tourists often do
they know more of local history
than the people who now run the show

TO MY DAUGHTER

Do you remember the turtle? I've forgotten
his name. His shell was cracked when we found him on the road
by the lake. Some Massachusetts kid had run his truck
over him. It was October and we took him
home with us to the city. He spent the winter
on a rock in a fish tank in a heated
apartment. We bought him tiny goldfish to eat.
He preferred tuna salad on a piece of lettuce.
The goldfish grew and became too big for him
to eat. Then they needed a fish tank of their own.
The following spring, on an April morning,
we returned the turtle to the lake and watched him swim.
We kept the tank of goldfish for several years.
Zachary was the snake. What was the turtle's name?

NEWLYWEDS

The newlyweds floated face down
in about three feet of water
        off Cape Cod.

They watched life on the sandy floor —
shrimps and big red starfish — through their
        snorkel masks.

She saw a small body and long
legs with weed growing on them — a
        spider crab.

It scuttled beneath her and she
jumped up and pulled the mask off her
        face and screamed.

God! It almost touched me! she wailed.
As they saw her clutch herself and
        wade ashore

swimmers abandoned the water
and lifeguards eyed the surface for
        telltale fins.

YOU CANOE

and stop
on a lake top
and look down into the clear deeps
as far as sunlight penetrates
and see
innumerable
struggling things
and little fish looking up at you
and you keep still
so long
the birds hidden in the shoreline trees
forget you are alive and go back
to doing the things they were doing
before you arrived

AFLOAT

High overhead I heard the traffic on the bridge
indistinctly through the fog but I saw nothing.

Ahab at the wheel of his big white motor yacht
his wife and guests below were playing cards.

He said what he was doing had less risk
than anchoring and waiting for the fog to thin

and chance being hit. Besides he had to appear
in court tomorrow morning or find a reason

the judge would accept. A bell pealed clearly
through absorbent fog its buoy lifted

on our wake. Behind us and out to sea
a groaner called like a sleepy walrus.

Ahab peered ahead. I poured scotch on rocks.
He had radar, charts, satellite positioning.

I said I'd stand in the prow and wave if I saw
anything. I did not expect to sight

the side of a house and some coniferous trees
directly in our path. Through its picture window

I saw mom, pop and two kids watch television
from a couch and turn their faces in unison

to look at us. Ahab swung the craft to starboard
of the tiny island with its lone summer house

and we were gone from their window view in moments
vanished into atmospheric interference.

PISSARRO IN MASSACHUSETTS

In the Sterling and Francine Clark Art Institute
near Williamstown in Massachusetts (the Berkshires)
you can see how Camille Pissarro liked to paint
industry's incursions into agriculture —
chimneys belching puffy smoke from small factories
that are quite plainly making only small headway
against the pasturelands festooned with wildflowers.

From Mount Greylock's nearby summit, the highest point
in Massachusetts, once walked by Mr. Thoreau,
      you can look down at a wooded valley
      and see an old New England mill town
      rest on its river, the waterwheels gone,
      the tall redbrick factory chimneys
            as empty as church spires.

      Trees, once downed by the sweating Puritans,
      have invaded the fields and now stand tall
in the smokeless air of the picturesque valley.

Would Pissarro jump on a bus to New York
      today or would he stay to watch
            on goldenrod
      brown velvet bordered by blue beads
            mourning cloaks
            open their wings?

STANLEY KUNITZ GARDENING

Reading things in his early nineties
Stanley Kunitz mentioned gardening,
how he found it difficult to bend
at his age, how he no longer worked
on his knees for any length of time.

He solved these problems by lying down
among the plants he needed to tend
and working in a prone position.

All went well until an ambulance
arrived one day and paramedics
held and secured him on a stretcher.

When Kunitz claimed that nothing was wrong
the emergency room doctor said,
 "You were reported lying face down
in flowers, twitching convulsively."
"I was weeding," the poet explained.

WINTER FIELD

A small dark figure
walks across
a distant snowy field

Snow is visible
through the trees
leafless on the ditches

The small dark figure
moves slowly
across the distant field

TOUR

Only rarely out of Connecticut,
she'd visit four European cities
in eight days with two friends and backpacking
stay in hostels. On her return, I asked
how much she liked Amsterdam. Great, with all
the Australian guys she met. Brussels too
and Paris. London was best. Some real
cool Australian guys at the hostel there.

PHOTO OPPORTUNITY

City women see an old bull moose
eating grass by the side of the road,
leave their car and approach real slow

so as not to frighten him. You first,
I'll take your picture, and then my turn.
The other picks some flowers she thinks

the moose might like to chew and holds them
out to him as she gets near. She says,
He's almost twice as big as our car.

He's smiling, the photo shooter claims
and she takes a shot. A state trooper
eases to a halt at a distance.

Once out of his car, he draws his gun.
Don't turn around, he calls. Walk backward
to the sound of my voice. They both turn

and stare. OK, he says, move slowly
toward me. They ask, What did we do?
They do not put their hands in the air.

You crazy bitches want to have me
killed? A driver passing phoned on this.
Jump in your car and get out of here.

Yes, the moose gazes into the lens
with what could be called a smile, and next
to his head a woman waves her hand.

ALPACAS

Jan Dekker of Vriezenveen, who showed us
the birds in his aviary, has had five
of his seventeen alpacas stolen.
He may find them because they remain an
unusual beast in the Netherlands.

Surprised to see alpacas in Vermont,
always one in a flock of sheep, I hear
an alpaca bonds with sheep and thinks of
itself as one, protecting lambs and ewes
from coyotes. They kick and bite, and when
coyotes get their scent they keep away.
Are they alpacas or are they llamas?

These are not the remnant flocks of sheep of
New England farmers, but rustic projects
of Wall Street refugees. With wealth and taste,
they choose rare breeds (each flock with resident
llama or alpaca) and they produce
astonishing cheeses that can be found
elsewhere only in Auvergne and Savoy.

In the New England countryside I buy
whole cheese, by which I mean unpasteurized.
But you won't get it if you ask for it.
Hold up a segment of commercial cheese
and say, Don't you have any local cheese?
With those code words, they nearly always do.

IN NORTH EGREMONT

A New England village
sedate geometry,
before all the numbing
flowerbed coziness
was inflicted on it,
may have provided balm
for riot and hardship
and pioneer life in
the seventeen hundreds.

A massive hardwood tree
knocked over in a storm
leans against three stories
of elegant clapboard
within an undisturbed
white-painted picket fence.

I have no doubt the tree
on losing its balance
and feeling that it was
uncomfortably close
to its neighboring house
apologetically
reached out tender branches
that snapped and fell and lie
on the ground at our feet.

Look how gently the trunk
rests against the modest
expertly carpentered
sedate exterior
with no broken windows
and few marks on the skin.

NAUSET BEACH

Shrapnel left big scars across his chest.
On Cape Cod he sat in marram grass
on a dune
a little way from the crowded beach.
A small girl, holding her mother's hand
on their way to the water, said in
a loud voice,
Tell me what happened to that man's chest.
Her mother tried to pull her away.
He told them,
I fell asleep in long grass like this
and a man on a motor mower
did not see me.
Afterward he slept in the long grass.
When he woke
five pairs of examining eyes looked
down on him.
The small girl had brought some friends and he
heard her tell them in a teacher's voice:
He fell asleep in long grass like this
and a man on a motor mower
did not see him.

WINGED SPIRIT

The thing unnerved old New Englanders:
an owl in flight turns its head to gaze
in your face and exchanges a glance
like someone you once knew long ago
and then the owl flies away from you
with absolutely silent wing beats

EARLY SUMMER MORNINGS

1
A camera operator told me
that on a sunny June morning in New England
she shot the spring part of a TV commercial,
a new couple in a new car
in maple woods in a valley.

She was told the next shoot, the part in fall,
was scheduled for early the next morning.

Another sunny June morning in New England
but instead of yesterday's green leafs of maple
she saw October brown, lemon yellow,
arterial crimson and dozens of colors
in a leaf peeper's autumnal panorama.

Workers in cherry pickers still applied
finishing touches from aerosol cans.

They brought in a crew from Los Angeles,
a production person said disapprovingly.

2
Claude Monet to Alice Hoschede,
Fresselines, 9 May 1889

I'm overjoyed, having unexpectedly been granted
permission to remove the leaves from that oak tree.
It was quite a business bringing sufficiently long
ladders into the ravine. Anyway it's done now,
two men having worked on it since yesterday.
Isn't it the final straw to be finishing a winter
landscape at this time of year.

IN A STRANGE LAND

After watching the ball game in Boston
he went to some bars with his friends who were

interchangeable white American
and they just laughed when people hassled him.

He was brown but there were blacks and other
Latinos and no one was hassling them.

What could all these people have against him?
How did they know he was Dominican?

Finally one of his friends said to him:
You are wearing a New York Yankees cap.

FIRST SNOWMAN

Newly moved to Boston from Los Angeles,
the nine-year-old built his first ever snowman.

Released to play, his dog, a black labrador,
out of exuberance destroyed the snowman.

The kid broke into tears, regressing in age.
His mother guessed he would long remember this

and one day tell his grandchildren how his dog
knocked down his newbuilt snowman when he was nine.

SOME NEW ENGLAND BUTTERFLIES

Variegated Fritillary
A restless nomad, given to wide travels

Silver-Bordered Fritillary
Partial to wetland edges and damp clearings

Meadow Fritillary
Low meandering flight

Harris's Checkerspot
Caterpillars form communal webs on flat-topped white aster

Question Mark
A small silver ? on the underside hindwing

Eastern Comma
A small silver , on the underside hindwing

Mourning Cloak
Awakens briefly from hibernation on warm winter days

Milbert's Tortoiseshell
In moist habitats near nettles

Red Admiral
Males territorial

Common Buckeye
A widespread wanderer

Pearl Crescent
Often basks with open wings

Baltimore Checkerspot
Toxic to predators, with shallow rapid wingbeats

Viceroy
Caterpillar resembles bird dropping

Common Wood-Nymph
A large strong-flying satyr of brushy fields and wood edges

4

SAVANNAH IN JULY

Mosquitoes bite downtown, wet and heavy air
feeds Spanish moss that droops off live oak branches
on period squares, each graced with monuments:

John Wesley in Episcopalian garb,
a railroad man, a general and his son,
an Indian who befriended Englishmen

and so on. The ornate bandstand in one square
repeated in another, or so I think
until I notice the same wino in it.

An old woman smiles at the pink-flowered trees,
the name of which she cannot recall just now,
but what a mess they make, petals everywhere.

HEADSTONES WITH
AN IRISH NAME

Beneath Savannah myrtle
two stones independent stand
side by side, identical
but for symbols carved on top:
hers a papist IHS,
a masonic compass, his.

ALLIGATOR

noses along
the water top

knobby body
parts the lilies

its tail moving
from side to side

reptile propelled
in no hurry

EGRETS

Egrets on the estuary elegantly
            in white-detergent plumes pick their way
      on tidal mud flats.

Dozens rise brilliantly white against the dark clouds
            their intensity of whiteness
      a forecast of rain.

The fashions changed in ladies' hats and boas
            the scatter guns of plume hunters
      hang in museums.

A lone egret stands long-legged on a cow's rump
            the cow seems glad of the company
      twitching its ears at flies.

As the cow moves through the meadow grass the egret
            runs alongside gobbling insects
      raised by the cow's hooves.

The earth is being scraped free of grass and trees
            to widen a Georgia road
      slowly cars roll by.

      Frantic egrets stab
            worms in the dirt and run in flocks
inches from the flattening tracks of heavy machines.

DISTANT FUNNEL

The road straight to the horizon,
a known number of miles away
when you're at sea. The tornado —
this is deep inland — is slightly
left of the road and wider than
both lanes, probably impressive
in size. Its anvil cloud points right.
On the left hand side there's blue sky,
making the amber atmosphere
look sinister. You know your end
will not be as pretty as this.

HOTHOUSE GERANIUMS

turn the tornado
funnel pink

PORTAVANT INDIAN MOUND

A mound of shell midden by the seashore,
tallest in Tampa Bay and area,
sprouting trees and ferns, by the mangrove edge
of the river mouth, topped by a fallen
chimney and concrete rainwater cistern.
Two interrupted rows of royal palms
line a path of broken shells to water.

Indians made a deliberate mound.
The man who built the vanished house on top
was loosed from a Union jail. His daughter
was born in this pioneer place. They moved.
A man whose name is now misspelled built the
cistern and grew citrus trees, two of which
still fruit. Then came the loving pair who set
the two wandering lines of royal palms
down to water, and they repaired the house.
She swam to rescue him and both here drowned
in the mouth of the Manatee river.

A boardwalk protects the mound. The state cuts
invasive trees to help native species.

JEFF CLIMBS OUT AND WALKS AWAY

In the Budweiser Shootout
at Daytona Beach with three
laps to go Jeff Gordon is
blocked by Kyle Bush and Gordon
taps his left rear fender and
pushes Bush off the track but
loses control, goes sideways,
gets hit and lifted into
the air, flips, end over end
to the grass inside the track
and instead of settling down
the car bucks, shudders and jumps
like a fish hung on a line,
expends the stored energy
you hear about in physics
before flopping on its roof,
only its wheels still moving

ALABAMA, 1964

There were things I still
did not understand.

Like all diners
where buses stopped
on interstates
it was integrated.

One end however
looked segregated.

I asked the black man
eating next to me
at the counter,
"Why do they eat down there?"

A white counterman
stood opposite me.

"This one," he said,
pointing to the black man
sitting next to me,
"leaves around here
on the bus with you.
Those ones," he said,
pointing to the black men
crowded at the end
of the diner,
"live around here
after dark."

"Now I know," I said.

"Now you know,"
he confirmed, evenly.

COUNTRY TRAFFIC

Not paying attention
in a traffic delay,
I rear end a pickup,
hardly more than a tap.

Confederate decal,
long gun in the gun rack,
long faces unshaven,
blue eyes, might be brothers.

The driver slow mumbles,
I was wondering if
you done it on purpose.
I tell him I didn't.

His brother assures me,
On the farm we get hit
by mad hogs that weigh more
than any Toyota.

STATUE

Her old house adjoins
a cemetery.

From her upstairs bedroom window
by the light of early morning
a stone angel with folded wings
appears to stand in her back yard.

One hand clasps its heart,
the other points at
tomato plants or
possibly the weeds.

PERENNIAL WEED

Beneath the concrete surface
lies a reinforcing mesh of steel.

On the smooth cheek of concrete
only mold can cling,

black and green molds whose fingers
insinuate between the particles.

Mold can do nothing to lift
my spirits, unlike an unnamed plant

squirting out of a deep crack
that given time will shoulder aside

the massive blocks oppressing
its stem and its roots.

EASTERN SHORE

Three men working on a county road,
they would know.
But they didn't, they said they never
heard of the house we were looking for.
I showed them the map in the guidebook,
the old house must be near where we stood.
They shook their heads.
Then they looked at the guidebook's cover,
a WPA travel guide
published in the late 1930s.
One said, You're on the wrong county road,
they changed the route numbers years ago.
Another said,
I know now which house you're looking for,
it burned down long before I was born.
More than forty years ago, I guessed.
The two saw things that made them laugh as
they turned pages.
The third man quietly looked at us.

INSIDE LOOKING OUT, OUTSIDE LOOKING IN

Snowy egrets on delicate legs
walk in the marsh, picking here and there
with narrow bills like ladies shopping,
watched by us inside a Chevrolet,
windows up, not because of urban
instincts but because of mosquitoes
knocking their heads against the glass, their
eyes hungrily looking in at us
like things from Night of the Living Dead
knowing what we are (skin-covered blood),
and we believe they may be hatching
a new mosquitoey strategy
to get inside and eat us alive

5

INDIAN GUIDE

Walpole Island Ojibwa,
Woody slapped at the flies and said how
he worked as a guide and took
groups of Ford executives hunting.

The men from Detroit and he
flew far north one time in a floatplane,
touched down on a pine-edged lake
and trekked into the trackless forest.

Woody had never before
been in a genuine wilderness.

They wandered for hours, told jokes
and had a very good time in there —
shot at anything that moved.

The sun got low ... they looked at Woody
and Woody looked back at them.

Then it dawned on him they thought of him
as instinctive pathfinder
who, no matter how spun, would point home.

He raised a palm to show peace
and said, with wooden face, Follow me.

Although they saw the humor
they believed and followed. On his part
Woody realized he had
marked the landmarks as they expected.

HIS UNCLE

He remembered leaving wild berries outside the door
and hoping the old man would think ghosts had left them there
and dragging by its tail a whole salmon as a gift
and hearing the rambling stories of the potlatch times
when the old man's father saw the things he told his son.

This was while he was still a boy and called the old man
uncle although not sure he was his father's brother —
if he was he was very much older and never,
unlike them, left the coastal village of their people
and this was where the anthropologists came to them.

While the old man was still a middling young man between
world wars, people said about the old man's father that
he had revealed to anthropologists things about
their people that these outsiders should never have heard
and had concocted stories for pay that were not true.

The old man always only laughed at that and said in
those days his father drank a lot and spent the money
on whiskey and beer, and often had no idea
what he had said but could remember having mixed up
secret things about their people with stuff he made up.

The people of older generations, when they heard
the things written by anthropologists about them,
laughed when the old man's father's jokes and imaginings
took over from real true things about their people,
concealing things so that they alone knew which were which.

When they heard in the city that the old man had died
his father left a plate of food in a flower bed
in case his journeying spirit came by to bid them
farewell, and his younger sisters and brothers grew still
the next morning when they saw that the plate was licked clean.

FAMILY VISIT

On a sailboat bobbing on a choppy bay
a rope is making a metallic
sound against the aluminum mast,
which brings me back to the early morning hours,
years ago, on a wood porch attached
to a mobile home, on a stifling humid
night on an Ontario reservation.
I had gone to sleep at ten p.m.,
like everyone else. I stood outside at four
smoking and looking up at the stars
in total darkness, total silence.

A thing making that metallic sound
passed where I knew the dirt road to be,
a dozen yards from me in darkness —
I heard no other sound but clanking
of rope on an aluminum mast
on a choppy bay on this windless
stifling night in a place at least fifty miles
from the nearest standing body of water.
I thought of owls, nighthawks and nightjars,
nocturnal birds swooping low over the dirt
roads, making that peculiar sound.

At breakfast with my wife's family
next morning I asked what might have made
the metallic sound that had passed up
and down the dirt road several times
before fading. This caused a silence
at the long table. What had the white man (me)
done now? An elderly cousin said
my wife's grandfather rode a sled that was pulled
by a horse. It was silent and fast
over snow, and so to give warning
he tied a cowbell to the harness.

It was true we had searched for his grave
the day before in the neglected graveyard
among fallen trees and heavy brush.
At the place, when she was still a child,
my wife half remembered he was laid,
she placed chocolate and cigarettes
and I poured whiskey. Now he had visited —
and I had not woken her in time,
a new grievance added to her store,
because somehow she knew he would not come back
again, lost now to her forever.

WAR CRY

Today is a good day to die,
            the Lakota said,
meaning, I think, you had taken time out
            to confront, if not befriend,
the shades that linger in your spirit life
            and shake you awake
when you hide under the eagle wing of sleep.

Do the grandmothers smile at you,
            the grandfathers nod,
when you journey to places
            where the vanished rule?

PROTEST

Was it in Colorado in the nineteen seventies
that an American Indian Movement activist,
after the state-sanctioned and university-sponsored
archeological desecration of ancient graves,
conducted a dig in a suburban cemetery?

A helper, committed in politics but by nature
a traditionalist, told the police they had arrived
exactly on time to stop an argument on whether
to walk away or dig all the way and repeat the crime.

AN ANTHROPOLOGIST COMES FULL CIRCLE

He went to Zuni Pueblo
to compile a Zuni dictionary
as a postgraduate student helper.

Much of the time he listened
to the words and phrases of old people,
the few who spoke an old form of Zuni.

Back in the nineteen twenties
before convenient mobile recording
he noted everything in fountain pen.

In a year he discovered
before returning to his school back east
he had an aptitude for the language.

He moved to other fields
in anthropology, had what is called
a long and distinguished teaching career.

On retirement he thought back
to his early days in New Mexico
and drove there with his wife of many years

who had been listening
to his stories about those early days
for many years and expected the worst.

When he tried his Zuni
people smiled and understood what he said,
then several serious Zuni men

came to their motel
to say the people had been listening,
word had gone around, they had come to hear

he was one of the few
people who could still speak the old Zuni
and would he mind if they recorded him?

BEFORE INTERCONTINENTAL MISSILES

The early warning radars strung inside
the Arctic Circle could provide three hours
to hide yourself from nuclear bombers
approaching America by the Pole.
A cousin spent four winter months in an

aluminum igloo packed with radar,
radio transmitters, generators,
fuel and supplies, alone because one
person could handle it better than two.
He had heat and food and plenty to do,

although he did not need to keep alert
for overflying Soviet aircraft
since long-distance radio transmission
of radar would waken America.
Snow fell, wind howled, daylight lasted an hour,

he heard taps on the igloo's metal skin
and he thought it might be a polar bear
but when he heard a shout he raised the hatch.
The Eskimo fed his dog team and drank
Coca Cola, smoked, chatted, slept a while

and left. My cousin could talk anytime
for any length by radio, mostly
to women, who sometimes cleverly placed
questions about his emotional state.
A woman with a velvet voice asked if

it had occurred to him the Eskimo
might only be a hallucination –
after all he was in a snowy waste,
below zero, about two hundred miles
from the nearest human settlement, in

an almost invisible white igloo.
He wondered what he might say after one
arrived with a dog pack a week later
and claimed he would only stop long enough
for a Coke, a smoke and to feed his dogs.

The skies remained clear of attacking craft
and minute by minute the days lengthened.
One, sometimes two, came almost every week.
He asked but never learned from where they came
and they never said where they were going.

IN GALLUP

The train is moving at more
than twice your walking pace
and perhaps even faster.

Its long sad whistle warns that
this iron horse on its twin rails
is coming through the town.

A tall man who wears
a hat with an eagle feather
resting in the brim
saunters across the tracks.

I see him from where I have parked
outside a pawnshop
that sells museum-quality
squashblossom necklaces.

I watch as he walks
away from me into the path
of the oncoming train.

The diesel locomotive hauls
a quarter mile of freight cars and
sounds its long sad whistle
but is not slowing down.

The tall man ambles onward
across the pair of rails
on which the train is running.

No smokestack or cowcatcher,
the locomotive is plain
utilitarian
everyday anonymous.

He pays it no more heed
than if he stood in the path of
a charging armadillo.

The diesel's flat face
touches his buckskin coat as
he unhurriedly lifts a boot
over a glistening rail.

A bullfight crowd would yell
at the close pass between
train wheel and boot heel.

But no one watches – only me
invisible in my car
and the engineer who pulls
the long sad whistle.

SEPTEMBER 6

I put a plate of food on the table
for the hungry spirit of my dead wife

the day of her first anniversary
according to Delaware tradition.

She has not touched the food I have served her
but we will not argue about that now.

6

LAKE SHORE

Touched by the wind in odd patches of ripples,
the lake is calm, the opposite shore hazy.

On the grass bank a man is supine, hat dropped
over his face. Beside him a woman reads,

showing her arms to the sun. A line stretches
taut from a rod to the lake depths. The woman

looks up. A thing slaps in the grass at my feet,
making me jump — a gasping silver-scaled fish.

THE FEAST OF ST. FILOMENA

Only minutes after darkness fell on Pennsylvania
we thought that we might spend the night at some motel
in this small town, which seemed unpretentious and unthreatening.

I stopped the car to make way for a procession
of hundreds of people holding flaming candles
and carrying placards of babies in the flickering light.

"They're Catholics," I said and waited for the penny to drop
but she was enchanted by the sight of so many people
singing and walking peaceably through the small town.

"What's it for?" she asked. I told her about St. Filomena,
the teenage nun in Italy who saved babies from the plague
and who has been honored for centuries all over the world.

My task now was to get her out of town before
she realized who these singing people were and
jumped from the car to scream at them about the rights of women.

The procession of candlelit singers through town
wended its way to the steps of a floodlit church
and I waited fifty miles before I told her the truth about St. Filomena.

LOOKING FOR WALTER

I will not say Walter had disappeared.
I hadn't heard from him in many months
and his friends had not met or talked to him,
but too soon to claim he had disappeared.

On the turnpike upstate one day we took
the exit for the town in which he lived.
I had come here once before for an hour
and remembered where his yellow house stood,
carpenter gothic with gingerbread trim
like all homes in this web of empty streets.
Where Walter's house had stood, a chain link fence
enclosed an area of broken stone.
I asked someone, What happened to the house?
That's always been here, she said, though the fence
looked recently erected. Nobody
knew Walter – at least that was what they said.

A long-tooth bartender poured us draft beer.
No one there admitted knowing Walter.
Person by person, insidiously,
the undead had taken over the town.
Walter had resisted friendly offers.
By now no untainted people remained.
Missionaries were already moving
in twos and threes to other local towns.
No one said a word. The beer tasted strange.
Would we escape this place in human form?

SHOP TALK

When I heard that many there would be
professional gardeners
I expected talk to be about
flora with Latin names.

If there was any dominant theme
it was their painful knees
and what it was best to kneel upon:
knee pads or folded sacks.

THE JOY OF GARDENING

He planted lettuce behind the house
and erected chicken wire head high.

Weeks later he saw a whitetail doe
clear the chicken wire without a run.

Her fawn cleared it in a standing jump.
He watched them enjoy the young lettuce.

HATE GROUPS

In a 2016 map published
by the Southern Poverty Law Center
with symbols representing the locations
of active hate groups in the United States
southern states are thickly coated in symbols,
Alaska and Hawaii have none,
the northwestern states have very few
(which I think of as crawling in yokels
protecting hideouts with automatic rifles),
while wilderness-free little New Jersey
festers in symbols for the Ku Klux Klan,
Racist Skinheads, White Nationalists, Neo-Nazis,
Neo-Confederates and Christian Identity.
As they say on television news: who knew?

A LONG RIDE NORTH

For family reasons
a guy in Texas had to
go to upstate New York
near the Canadian border.

He'd lost his driver's license,
he'd very little money
but he owned a good horse
and decided to ride north.

This he did, and I thought there
might be a book in it or
a magazine article
about happenings on the way.

He'd crossed the Mississippi
and the Hudson as well as
major interstate highways,
had probably made use of

mountains, parks and country lanes
anywhere he could find them
and he must have had some
interesting interactions

with motorists, cops, rangers
and some curious people
who wanted information
about this man on a horse.

I telephoned him upstate
at the family place
and while I'd say he was not
a yup and nope kind of guy

I would not say that he was
verbally effusive –
he had no problems on the ride
and nothing much had happened.

No one ever asked him where
he and the horse were going
or where they were coming from,
not even cops or rangers,

and he guessed that most people
must have assumed he was from
some local stable out for
a ride in the traffic.

When he tied the horse outside
a fast food place some people
always worried it might kick
or scratch the paint of their cars.

He took care not to tire the horse
and found grass and fresh water
and a big tree or rock where
he could shelter for the night.

All in all, he'd say it was
an uneventful journey
and when his horse was rested
they would head back to Texas.

OVERCAST

Snow lay a few inches deep across miles
of level farmland in Ontario.

Whatever it was they raised did not
need to be fenced in – an expanse of snow,
the farmhouses here and there without a tree
or bush, houses that might have been charming
a hundred years ago before huge sheds
were erected next to them to hold
giant machines for agribusiness
and big drums for diesel or pesticides.

Without snow tires or chains, I followed
a single pair of tracks on the lonely road.

I caught up with the truck making these tracks
and doing about thirty miles an hour.
I followed since there was nothing else to do.
He stopped at a farmhouse and walked back to me.
I live here, he said and glanced at
my New York plates. You've followed me across
my fields. Please leave. I retraced our tire tracks.
He watched until I was off his land.

7

DELTA FLIGHT 708

In the seat in front of me
a guy in baseball cap and fancy audio gear
        pulls down the window shade and
                I push it up.

He claims the light interferes
with viewing his seat-back screen and there's nothing for me
        to see out the plane window
                except some clouds.

I say he'd be better off
watching clouds than Britney Spears videos, which hits hard.
        Come on, I wasn't watching
                no Britney Spears,

he insists, to which I say,
I'm not criticizing you, it's none of my business
        what you watch. He seems to sink
                low in his seat.

In a while I hear him say,
Anyway there are no Britney Spears videos here.
        No more talk of window shades.
                I watch the clouds.

REDEYE WINDOW SEAT

Somewhere over perhaps Iowa
at two in the morning the dark sea
is broken by a township of lights.

Through the blurred plastic of the window
a line of parallel lights below
marks the length of Main Street. No traffic.

Where is there to go in Iowa
at two in the morning? I see an
empty illuminated car park.

Then the dark sea closes in again.
After time and distance it appears:
a light, solitary in the gloom.

What is it doing alone down there
at two in the morning? Far too big
to be a kitchen or bedside lamp.

It has to be a light in a yard
and someone has let it burn all night
and this is the second time this week.

REPELLENT

A Seven-Eleven store
kept open around the clock
heard complaints from customers
of youths lingering outside.

Bright lights did not repel them.

One man claimed he knew what would.

Play Mozart very softly
nonstop on outside speakers
and no self-respecting dude
will be caught dead for a mile.

ELLINGTON IN IOWA

Even now, many years later,
when he returns to his hometown
deep in the corn of Iowa
some people always remember
one time he was the high school kid
who brought Duke Ellington to town.

The bus from Chicago arrived
outside the graduation dance
and he recalls the band members
examining their surroundings,
polite and elegantly dressed,
among farm kids in Sunday best.

Then the band played and the kids danced
and the night happened that people
remember all these years later.
Mr. Ellington stayed formal
but as he left he shook their hands
and said this is my kind of town.

IN SEARCH OF POLYGAMISTS

I wanted to see polygamists
and left the bus at Salt Lake City.

It took only a short time to find
that Mormons looked much the same as me.

Then I saw people who seemed to fit
expectations of polygamy.

I followed them to another bus
and sat beside a man clothed like

Abraham Lincoln. The women could
have stepped out of an old Dutch painting.

He said I had made a big mistake
in thinking they were polygamists –

polygamists looked the same as me,
not them. At a lonely town, he asked

if I thought it strange that such a place
had so many large houses, each with

several independent doorways.
I said thank you and got off the bus.

I wanted to see polygamists,
even if they looked the same as me.

A LONE FLAMINGO

A lone flamingo, on long legs, neck extended,
moved its beak from side to side to filter brine shrimp
in the shallows, unselfconscious among the gulls,
a blot of pink in the extensive salty grays.

Wings unclipped, escapee from an aviary,
wintering on the Great Salt Lake for sixteen years,
known to the public as Pink Floyd, this flamingo
disappeared each summer no one knew where or why.

Where could a bright plumaged five foot exotic hide?
In plain sight. When anyone came in view Pink Floyd
stood motionless on some lawn among the many
ornamental life size plastic pink flamingos.

FUN BISON FACTS

Despite a huge head and thick skull
a bison can run
up to 35 miles per hour.

At Yellowstone Park
bison injure more visitors
than grizzly bears do.

The Morton County Sheriff's Department
recounted how Standing Rock protestors
against the Dakota Access Pipeline
rode on horseback behind a bison herd
to stampede it toward law enforcement.

You know they knew what the TV would say –
a posse of white dudes fighting the Sioux
got themselves run over by buffalo.

ARIZONA AFTERNOON

The sky has the mild featureless blue
of an old woman's eyes. The white stucco
is blinding. Today the Superstition Mountains
look red and contorted. A kid on a bike
beyond the motel swimming pool
is selling drugs. He hasn't noticed how,
coiled and silent, the wall-mounted
camera monitors him.

MOGOLLON RIM

Atop
an inland cliff looking out on a sea of pines

a dirt road
wanders hour after hour
from sunup to sundown

merciless.
Thunderheads in full sail blow across the blue sky.

Out here
miles from anywhere
in Arizona

wilderness
hard to believe someone dumped industrial waste.

I leave the car,
feeling righteous
indignation, and look

all around me
at thousands of white plastic spheres smaller than golf balls.

I pick one up:
it is heavy and solid ice,
a stone fallen minutes ago.

Only now do
they begin to steam in the afternoon heat.

REAL-WORLD SCENE

A Roman poet
on a visit to Nevada,
foreseeing
the doom of civilization
on the future light cone of space-time,
soundlessly
as the ultrasonic postejaculatory song of the male rat
folds his tent
and moves away across colossal ruins
of wind-blown desert sand

8

RUBY BEACH

After the sun, like egg yolk
separating from albumin,
slips over the edge
of the Pacific rim,
from the beach we climb
the forest path
on which the huge yellow
slugs with black spots
are easier to avoid
in fading light
than dark red ones
glistening like cabernet

IMPRESSION

Had Monet a field
of multicolored
Washington dahlias
the man would have chucked
his pond and lilies.

Mendel would have traded
sweet peas, and Darwin his
Galapagos finches.

Vincent would have put
his peaceful absinthe
on the zinc counter
and swung at Gauguin.

FRIDAY

This morning I woke alone,
empty and full of fear.

What I do now, I decided,
must not be dictated by my fear.

Resisting the urge to lose myself
in work, I reached instead

for my guitar and played
the few tunes I play tolerably.

As I hung the instrument back
on the nail in my bedroom wall,

sunlight hit the bare wood floor.

NORTHWEST FOREST

I call them hemlocks and redwoods,
trees that darken the afternoon
and make me remember the story of the man who left his car

and walked some yards into the woods
to take a leak and could not find
his way out again, the scattered and chewed bones presumed to be his,

in the twilight of these big trees
in which I feel like a swimmer
suddenly aware of marine possibilities underneath

my kicking legs and flashing skin,
no map, compass, food or water,
no things creeping toward me on furred belly except my own thoughts

URBAN PROBLEM

An old friend in Oakland
lives in a part of town
that's getting gentrified.

He looks back on the time
when nightly gunfire kept
the upwardly mobile
a neighborly distance.

Now he ponders maybe
handing out blanks to friends.

PONDEROSA

Ponderosa on a slope
of university grass
on a San Francisco hill,
the place they agreed to meet
if catastrophe occurs,
when his highrise office shakes
its contents into the streets,
when she drops her things and runs,
people flailing everywhere,
they will come to meet beneath
this big pine tree on this hill

ELEPHANT SEALS IN CALIFORNIA

1
No appointment in my name
to visit elephant seals.

Reservations must be made
at least a week in advance.

This is now the second year
I am being turned away.

2
Rangers closely supervise
small numbers of visitors

to keep them from disturbing
the breeding elephant seals

on an isolated beach
in protected wilderness.

3
Going south? a ranger asks.
Opposite the entrance gate

to the Hearst estate, you'll see
a colony overflow

just doing their thing roadside.
You don't have to leave your car.

4
Scarred, a bull elephant seal
guards his females on the beach.

Rising high on front flippers,
he points his snout in the air.

He makes a noise like water
circling down a metal drain.

HOME AND CASTLE

When I mentioned how Hearst in his castle
had a strict code of behavior for guests
and how you knew you had been caught and judged
when a chambermaid next morning unasked
began to pack your bags
                          a friend announced
anyone who visits her apartment
and steps out of line is out the door
no time lost and good for Mr. Hearst
the man knew how to run a castle

THEY HUNT TO EAT

1
At Ojai a coyote waits
in darkness in long grass by a dirt road
waits for our approaching headlights
to illuminate creatures scurrying
and when we stop he slinks away
I think not pleased we understand his game

2
The falcon knows the flakes of snow
break up his image in the eyes
of pigeons on the empty street
and glides on windswept pointed wings
at speed above the traffic lights
unseen until it is too late

MOUNTAIN FACE

The rock face stared back aggressive as if
it did not much care for the look of me.

Apart from conifer tufts and wrinkles
made by rock slides, the face was red and raw.

I thought I saw something move halfway up,
an animal that scampered on bare rock,

two of them. They might be cougars, bears, wolves.
Bighorn sheep were a possibility.

I focused my binoculars and groaned:
one wore a green shirt, and the other blue.

LITTLE FISHES

In early hatcheries
the fry lived in a pool,
over which a dead cow's
head was hung. The maggots
that devoured the cow's head
dropped off in the water
and became salmon food.

This taught the baby fish
to wait for food to drop
from the sky. They lost their
instinct to fear shadows
of predators above.

Mothers, remember this
when you are preparing
to feed your little ones.

HELP FOR VULTURES

You know the way that vultures soar
over wilderness and mountains
without expending a wing beat
for hour after hour at a time.

Think how a transmitter attached
to scaly leg or back feathers
could enable cell phone service
in areas where vultures hang.

This might help their reputation
and change our attitude to them.

BODYGUARD

Bodyguard to the stars
might seem an easy way
to make a buck, with sex
and other perks maybe.

Beautiful, ultra fit,
scampering among the
rocks west of Malibu,
trailed by her bodyguard ...

Flushed, overweight, a cop
off duty, flat-footed,
where she goes there he goes
and dreams of criminals.

TOOK A LOOK

He gave her the binoculars
to watch brown pelicans gliding
over Malibu onshore kelp.

She said, I think that surfer there
acts in a television show.

RAPPER GUNNED DOWN AT UPSCALE MALL

Dolla might have liked the posturing mockingbird
          perched on a cypress tip
only a few miles away from the Westside mall,
bending its evergreen apex under his weight
and loudly singing his territorial song:
the notes and phrases repeated up to six times,
his tone varied, vocabulary extensive.

Dolla arrived at LAX early that day
and he went with friends to the Beverly Center.
          He was shot in the head
near the La Cienega Boulevard entrance.
The LAPD later detained a man who
allegedly drove from the mall to LAX
in a rented silver Mercedes SUV.

The mockingbird sings in darkness, after midnight,
his impulse triggered perhaps by a backyard light
controlled by a motion detector, and he sings
before dawn in anticipation of the day
          and he sings all the day
with a vehemence that might exhaust a rapper,
answered by rivals on nearby eminences.

MANDATORY EVACUATION AT 3 A.M.

Mandatory evacuation,
the sheriff's deputy declares. You need to get
your things together and get
out of here.

The wind has changed, and nothing can hold
wind-driven flames. If they come off the mountainside
they will burn every one of
these houses.

I get my things together and load
the car. The sheriff's men cannot force me to leave.
The woman who lives next door
wonders if

I have any kind of fishing net.
She has collected her five cats and dog but she
will not leave her fish behind
in the pond,

not after hearing about the two
people who refused to leave and then were scalded
while immersed in their backyard
Jacuzzi.

QUAKE

It was nine minutes to five, Pacific time,
by the moving hands on the face of my watch,

in strength a high two or a low three,
an earth tremor that caused no damage

but certainly one that we noticed
as we stood in the kitchen doorway,

a helicopter floating in the sky
bright red as a tropical fish,

on television white domestic geese
called swans by the voiceover,

and it was exactly nine minutes to five
by the count displayed on her digital watch.

PINKELPONKERS

In bed in the early morning hours
I hear tiny footsteps on the roof
much too light for raccoon or possum
or their babies – and squirrels are not
nocturnal and no way would rats or
big mice run on a roof in moonlight.

You'd never know what might be out there
so near the San Gabriel mountains.

While there seem to be many they sound
by their feet reassuringly small.

They keep scampering and skittering
above my head and I cannot sleep.

Pull on shirt and jeans and barefoot make
my way in darkness out the door and
snap on yard light and quickly look up.

I see a rooftop bare: nothing there.

Daylight tells its logical story:
a sweet gum's long-stemmed clusters of fruit,
spiky balls turned hard and brown with age,
lie scattered by wind upon the ground
and overfill the plastic gutter.

SHORT TAKES OF MARLON BRANDO

EARLY
An actor returned to Dublin
from a months-long run in New York
said he threw a party before
leaving, in a Greenwich Village
walkup coldwater apartment.

Brando knocked on the door and asked
to come in. The actor said no,
he had to play by Dublin rules
(Bring a bottle or bring a girl)
and then closed the door in his face.

He showed again with a woman
on each arm and a case of scotch
on one shoulder, to loud applause.
Things like that mattered in those days.
It took Brando fourteen minutes.

LATE
A writer who moved from the crowd
into Jack Nicholson's kitchen
knew the hulk who entered a door
and who dragged in each hand a black
plastic bag across the wood floor.

One bag held grapefruit, one vodka.
Brando squeezed fruit, poured the vodka,
maybe knew there was a party
and in a while wandered out to
the darkness on Mulholland Drive.

HOLY FAMILY

Remember how the Fox News helicopter stalked
Britney Spears and baby in baby seat as she drove
midday local time on Route 5 and hung a U-turn

through a police gap in the divider and performed
a perfect semi ovoid at speed in the face
of six oncoming lanes of aroused voyagers.

How sharp the Hollywood druids were in pointing
a fingernail to what loomed in statistics for
a miraculously uninjured mother and child.

SANDWICH

I am in an East Coast hurry
for no particular reason.

Standing in line for a sandwich
at Ralphs, I am irritated
by a man I can only hear
ordering in a monotone
three sandwiches, each with something
added or taken away, one
with cress but without anchovy.

I look at the cause of delay.

Italians, Greeks and French are known
to care about ingredients
and this one is large and muscled
and coated in construction dust.

Time to think of the benefits
of Mediterranean food
with cress but without anchovy.

A PACK FORMS

Strange to see the five-year-olds
on their first baseball lesson
standing around and looking
every direction except
at the batter on home plate

but in an hour they all know
they are on opposing teams
and look in one direction
determined that while they play
the batter will go nowhere

BOB HOPE LIVES HERE

Celebrity home tour buses
in Beverly Hills often stopped
outside the dwelling of Bob Hope.

Often he obliged by taking,
in a dressing gown and slippers,
something out to a garbage can.

Bob knew only a great actor
could hold an audience spellbound
while disposing of kitchen waste.

FREEWAY

Six lanes at a gentle seventy,
hard to believe all these cars are bound
for driveways in front of modest homes,

they ease right and exit one by one,
others enter, keeping numbers up.

I think: No more exits. Stay in lane.
Mexico, wake up! We're headed south.

CAMINITO BRAVURA

Her heart went out to them,
the old pair in the building
she moved to, who took so long
even to leave the building,
assisting each other

and making sure they remembered
where they were going and had left
nothing behind, he holding the door open
for her, the door of the open-top

red Sixty-Eight Mustang it took them
five minutes to get into, and three seconds
to burn rubber on the driveway

A WALK NEAR GUATEMALA

I did not care when the Indian guide
I hired hired another Indian guide
out of what I was to pay him, saying
the new man was local, a thing I had
understood the original to be.

I think he is from the mountains where we
are going, he explained and politely
had me show the new guide my revolver.
The sight of the gun made him smile. They spoke
together in what may have been Nahuatl.

We got off the bus on the highway and
walked on a path along a mountain slope.
Children greeted us at small settlements
and from adults we purchased food and drink
In the doorways of tiny stone houses.

At one place the children did not greet us.
They ran around and continued their games
as if we were invisible to them.
The adults went inside and closed their doors
without having made eye contact with us.

My guides turned around and retreated back
the way we came, closely followed by me.
We must be off this mountain before dark,
one said. Both seemed genuinely frightened.
We waited on the highway for a bus.

Someone has been killed, the second guide judged.
These families fight with one another
and then keep a silence with those outside.
They think you must be a federal man
and we are not willing to die with you.

THE LOST FOOTSTEPS OF COL. FAWCETT

You do not walk today in the lost footsteps
of disappeared Fawcett, who knew where to find
a city of legend hid in the jungle
and who may have been hit by a blowgun dart
or have been trailed into the rainforest and
waylaid by needy thugs from a shantytown

You do not walk today in his lost footsteps
beneath long vines hanging from the canopy,
you drive a truck on dirt roads through remaining
ash and carbonized stems, it's slash and burn here
and no more worry about blowgun darts but
keep a watch for needy thugs from shantytowns

RIO

The white men on the raft in the Green River
shook their heads and fists at mounted Indians
who beckoned them to paddle toward the bank.

Then they heard the rapids before they saw them.

On a Rio street when a man shook his head
I nodded and turned back the way I had come.